Pre-Publication Praise for LAND IS A BIG DE...

"Inspiring a renewal of interest in Georgist ideas whose full ramifications are yet to be determined."
—Scott Alexander, author of Astral Codex Ten

"A really excellent overview of land wealth in America"
—Noah Smith, Economist

"Lars's work is intellectually fascinating and among the clearest and most compelling writing in support of land value taxes that I've seen."
—Vitalik Buterin, founder of Ethereum

"Why land matters more today than ever... and why economists, urbanists & everyone else need to take Henry George seriously."
—Richard Florida, co-founder of Bloomberg CityLab

"An absolutely wonderful summary of the economics of Henry George and land value taxes. Comprehensive but accessible, and above all fun!"
—Rethinking Economics

"Take the Georgist pill and read this."
—Arpit Gupta, author of Arpitrage newsletter

"Have you seen the cat? Whether or not Doucet converts you to Georgism, you'll come away with a new appreciation for how every economic system is built on the same resource: land."
—SlimeMoldTimeMold.com

Lars A. Doucet

LAND IS A BIG DEAL

Why rent is too high, wages too low, and what we can do about it

First Edition

Shack Simple Press

LAND IS A BIG DEAL
Copyright © 2022 by Lars A. Doucet

Shack Simple Press
601 Yorkshire Drive
College Station, TX 77845
https://www.shacksimplepress.com/

Land is a Big Deal / Lars A. Doucet, — 1st ed.
Paperback ISBN 979-8-9853225-2-1

Some of this material was originally published on astralcodexten.substack.com and gameofrent.com

Printed in USA

Dedication

For Emily

Table of Contents

Foreword(s)

This book began its life as a series of articles that struck a nerve online and became more popular than I could ever have imagined. To explain how we got from there to here, I asked two friends to lend some words of introduction for how this all came about, as well as the broader economic context in which this book was written.

—Lars A. Doucet

Who even writes forewords for books anymore? The only place I ever see forewords is in old texts, by some historian trying to explain the context in which the book was written. So in case anyone is reading this book a hundred or a thousand years in the future, here's the context.

In the 2020s, when this book was written, median USA rent had gone up 20% (in real terms) over twenty years. Houses were skyrocketing in price so consistently that large investment groups were snapping up much of the available stock. Leading newspapers (an archaic form of media sort of like a blog, but more pretentious) declared "the end of the American Dream of homeownership." An elderly man with period-atypical facial hair achieved national acclaim for founding a political party called "The Rent Is Too Damn High." Urban dwellers organized into factions with names like "NIMBYs" and "YIMBYs" to fight over whether the government should allow new houses to be built.

I was a blogger during this period, and hit on the idea of running a book review contest. After getting over a hundred entries, I decided to let readers vote on the best. The overwhelming winner was a Norwegian-Texan game designer I'd never heard of, who wrote a review of Henry George's "Progress And Poverty," which explained the reasons that housing was so expensive and set out a program for solving the problem. I gave him the prize of five thousand dollars (an archaic currency sort of like Bitcoin, but less useful for buying drugs) and expected never to hear about it again.

I was wrong. There's an old optical illusion where, if you stare at it long enough, the image of a cat suddenly jumps out, so obvious that you can't understand how you missed it before. The Georgists talk about their own movement in terms of "seeing the cat"—realizing the degree to which land affects the economy is a sudden perspective shift, surprising and irreversible. Lars' entry in my book review contest caused thousands of people to see the cat at once. It ended up getting 114,000 views, being shared hundreds times on Twitter (an archaic social media site sort of like voluntarily subjecting yourself to painful electric shocks, but more addictive), and inspiring a renewal of interest in Georgist ideas whose full ramifications are yet to be determined. One of those ramifications is this book.

The really frustrating thing about Georgism is the typical response from economists (an archaic profession kind of like an oracle, but less accurate). They say sure, it is a brilliant idea, it would solve a lot of problems—but it is a nonstarter for lack of political will to carry it out, so it is doomed. They make a good point. But you can solve lack of political will by building political will—the job Lars has set for himself here.

If you're reading this book in the distant future, I hope your society has found that this movement is not so hopeless after all. And if you're reading it in the present, I hope it inspires you to become a part of that change.

—Scott Alexander, author of Astral Codex Ten

It would only be a slight exaggeration to say that humanity's history is defined by a struggle over land. We find ourselves populating a 2-dimensional spherical surface with a fixed amount of territory. We did not create this territory (or at least, not most of it); thus, it represents the ultimate zero-sum game.

Land has value for many reasons. Some of it can be farmed. Some of it has useful minerals underneath it. Some pieces are close to valuable natural features like harbors. We've been fighting over these resources since the beginning of time. Individuals, tribes, nation-states and armies would try to kick each other off bits of land and claim ownership for themselves. Some of this is still going on.

Property rights help formalize and legitimize this forceful conquest. When you sell a piece of land to someone, you're participating in a chain of peaceful land sales that began at some point in the past with a violent seizure. Unlike property rights over a house or a corporation—things made via human effort and ingenuity—property rights over land has always carried a slight taint of violence. This is one reason why cries for economic justice often come in the form of calls to redistribute farmland from large landlords to small farmers, or to return land to its previous owners.

But this is not the only reason why land ownership has always been suspicious. Because in addition to natural resources, there's another key reason land has value—namely, its proximity to other land. If you build a house out in the middle of nowhere, it won't be worth a lot; if you build it right next to Central Park, it'll be worth millions of dollars, simply because it is situated close to a big cluster of valuable human activity.

Most of this value, too, is not created by the person who owns the land. People who were lucky enough to hold the title deeds to parcels of land in the middle of San Francisco in 1990 have seen their property values shoot up as successive booms in the information technology industry have turned their city into a high-tech business hub. Through no actions of their own, they have become rich.

This enrichment of landowners sucks value away from the workers and the businesses that created the economic value. San Francisco doesn't just have high land prices—it has astronomical rents, which appropriate value from workers and companies and hand it to lucky landlords. These unnecessary added costs make our economy less efficient and less productive. In recent years, some residents of these overpriced cities have begun to rebel against the zoning regimes and other regulations that restrict housing supply in order to bring rents down.

Meanwhile, economists have long searched for an elegant solution to the problems posed by land. The 19th-century scholar Henry George—himself a San Franciscan—believed that poverty itself was a result of unequal landownership, and came up with an innovative solution. George believed that taxing the value of land itself—rather than the structures or other improvements humans create on top of that land— would allow governments to relieve poverty, restore efficiency, and remedy injustice all in one stroke.

Surprisingly, more sophisticated analyses in later centuries bore the idea out. A land value tax, or LVT, has many theoretical virtues. Unlike income taxes, which can discourage people from working, an LVT wouldn't penalize any valuable activity—since humans (mostly) don't make land, they can't really make any less of it. Returning the proceeds from an LVT in the form of education, infrastructure construction, and reduced corporate taxes could encourage economic growth, while paying the revenues out with anti-poverty programs could create more equitable, livable cities.

So on paper, land value taxes are beautiful objects. But the technical challenges involved in implementing them— especially the thorny issue of assessing the value of land separately from the value of the buildings on top of it—are formidable. That's why believers in Henry George's big idea—who call themselves Georgists—have invested a lot of time and thought into figuring out how this might work. This book is part of that effort.

And it is important to remember that the quest to remedy the inherent injustice of landownership is not limited to debates over land value taxes. There are many other ideas to redistribute the benefits of land—agricultural land reform, government housing construction as in Singapore, and others.

Georgism, therefore, should be thought of as a broad movement—and one that didn't begin in the 19th century, but has been going on for as long as humans have been fighting over scraps of the map. Turning the inherently zero-sum-game of landownership into something that supports human equality and productivity is among our greatest challenges, and a dream that must never die.

—Noah Smith, Economist

1

What's the Deal with Land?

Popular economic debate is obsessed with just two things: Labor and Capital. Labor is the exertion of human beings, and Capital is the stored-up product of labor, transformed into tools, machines, and other useful things used to help produce more wealth. Labor and Capital each have their own dominant school of thought—Socialism and Capitalism, respectively—that have spent the last century sucking up all the oxygen and leaving little room for alternatives.

Proponents of Capital focus on topline Gross Domestic Product (GDP) and the stock market and support investment, capital formation, and business owners. Proponents of Labor focus on working conditions and compensation and support the health, education, welfare, and bargaining power of the people who do all the work. Crucially, we've been trained to see these two camps as fundamentally opposed—if we want to stimulate growth and economic progress, it means squeezing workers, and if we want to take care of workers it means accepting higher taxes, more barriers to starting and running a business, and a hit to overall economic growth.

But what if we've been missing out on a crucial piece of the puzzle, something that flips the entire script?

Take a look at this picture (Hayes, 2020):

Do you see the cat?

Nestled in the negative space between the tree's branches, the cat represents the hidden role of land that shapes the entire economy: once you've seen it, you can't un-see it. Land, and the policies that govern it, hold an incredible and largely forgotten power over our lives. When land is wasted and squandered, we get sky-high rents, oppressed workers, ruined businesses, depleted natural resources, a polluted earth, and an impoverished society.

Land is a big deal, and this book will explain the problem and what we can do to solve it.

PART I is a review and summary of *Progress and Poverty*, the seminal text concerning the land problem. That book was the magnum opus of 19th century American political economist and populist firebrand Henry George and was so popular in its time that many have claimed it outsold all other books except the Bible[1]. I explain and contextualize Henry George's philosophy—known today as Georgism or Geoism—for modern readers. Then, I lay out his proposed solution to the land problem: the "Land Value Tax," a tax on the annual rental value of land, but which excludes the value of all improvements, such as buildings.

Having established the problem and its solution, I then move

---

[1] The book's success is undeniable and widely attested, but a specific claim like this is hard to pin down. Various sources estimate *Progress & Poverty* sold 2 million copies worldwide over its lifetime (Mott, 1947) (Nock, 1933). To give that number some context, the US's population in 1879 was about 50 million, 15% of what it is today. I was unable to find reliable figures for 19th century Bible sales to compare against.

on to addressing critics. There are three common practical objections that newcomers to George's philosophy tend to raise: 1) that land just isn't an important part of the economy anymore, 2) that Land Value Tax will just be passed on to tenants and make everything more expensive, and 3) that even if all the theory is correct, unimproved land can't be accurately assessed in practice, so the whole project is doomed.

The next three parts address each of these objections in turn.

PART II empirically establishes that land is a big deal, not just in the 19th century, but even and especially today. First, I demonstrate that the chief component of sky-high urban real estate prices is due to land values, not buildings. Second, I collect and synthesize all the best estimates of America's total land values and demonstrate how a tax on the annual rental value of land could raise enormous sums of revenue sufficient to significantly offset or even replace existing sales, income, and capital taxes. Finally, I show the degree to which real estate has come to dominate bank lending, how housing has become the largest asset class in the world, and the degree to which land ownership is concentrated among the wealthy.

PART III lays out the empirical case for Land Value Tax not being passed on to tenants. I explain the theoretical basis for this and then provide empirical evidence showing the effects of Land Value Tax policies in the real world. It is often claimed that landlords will just raise rents in response to the tax, but not only are there strong theoretical reasons to doubt that claim, there is actual evidence from the real world that shows us that it doesn't happen.

PART IV evaluates the available methodology and current state of practice for assessing unimproved land values separately from buildings. I give an overview of established best practices, critique the status quo where it falls short, and present a sampling of the latest methods from the research literature that can improve upon the state of the art.

PART V concludes by reviewing all the evidence and practical case studies we've seen so far and charts a path forward for the work that lies ahead.

With the path now laid out before us, let us begin at the beginning with Henry George and his seminal work, *Progress and Poverty*.

PART I

Progress and Poverty

2

Henry George

In 1879, a man asked, "How come all this new economic development and industrialized technology hasn't eliminated poverty and oppression?" That man was Henry George, his answer came in the form of a book called Progress & Poverty, and this is a review of that book.

Henry George is variously known for leading an early movement that popularized Universal Basic Income, sporting a fancy beard while shouting "The Rent Is Too Damn High!" and inspiring a popular board game that was shamelessly ripped off and repackaged as Monopoly (Forsyth, 2021).

However, he didn't just write a book. He also ran for Mayor of New York City in 1886 (Brookhiser, 1993), beating out some obscure Republican named "Theodore Roosevelt," but ultimately losing to the favored candidate of Tammany Hall[2], who saw George's radical economic ideas as a threat to their well-oiled political machine. He ran again in 1897 but died just 4 days before the election, prompting a national outpouring of grief. According to Ralph Gabriel's Course of American Democratic Thought, in New York alone 200,000 people came to see his body lying in repose, half of whom had to be turned away (Gabriel, 1946). For context, that one

---

[2] The powerful and corrupt political machine that dominated New York politics in the 19th century.

crowd was roughly the size of 10% of the entire population of New York City at the time (Demographia, 2021).

I'm writing this book review for three reasons:

1.   George's arguments about land, labor, and capital present a fresh alternative to conventional ideas about "Capitalism" and "Socialism" (and whatever we mean by those on any given day).

2.   The book has timeless advice for navigating modern crises such as ever-rising rents, homelessness, and the NIMBY[3] vs. YIMBY[4] wars.

3.   This is a golden opportunity to shamelessly over-use the catchy phrase "By George!"

If I had to summarize George's book in a single sentence, I would put it this way: "Poverty and wealth disparity appear to be perversely linked with progress; The Rent is Too Damn High, and it is all because of land."

Progress and Poverty is quite readable compared to other 19th-century economic tomes but has a tendency to repeat

---

[3] "Not in My Back Yard." A derisive epithet for people who oppose more housing being built in their area.

[4] "Yes in My Back Yard." A self-applied epithet for people who intentionally counter NIMBY's by actively promoting more housing development in their area.

itself. This isn't without purpose—George goes to great pains not to be misunderstood; rather than expecting his readers to tease out the meaning of dense prose and spending the next century arguing with each other about what he "really meant," he goes on for pages and pages beating a single concept to absolute death, just to be sure.

As a 19th century treatise of *Political Economy*, the book doesn't match what a modern reader might expect from a book on *Economics* because it is not packed to the gills with charts, graphs, tables, and statistics (though it does provide a good number of citations and figures). Nevertheless, his argument was compelling enough to spawn an entire economic school of thought, known variously as Georgism or Geoism, that persists to this day.

Nowadays, Georgism gets slapped with the "heterodox" label, but it is still relevant enough to get the likes of Paul Krugman and Milton Friedman to grudgingly agree to key points, and Friedrich Hayek is alleged to have been inspired by it to pursue economics in the first place (Friedman, 1978) (Moore, 2017) (Andelson, 2003). Marx, on the other hand, wasn't a fan, seeing it as a last-ditch attempt "to save capitalist domination and indeed to establish it afresh on an even wider basis than its present one... [George] also has the repulsive presumption and arrogance which is displayed by all panacea-mongers without exception" (Marx, 1975). I guess you can't please everyone.

George spends the first few books of Volume I establishing terms and methodically tearing apart the prevailing economic theories of his day before presenting his own alternative theories about how the "three factors of production"—land, labor, and capital—relate to each other in the "laws of distribution." He then explains why the existing system causes poverty to advance alongside progress, and why we see industrial depressions. Then, he identifies the root cause of the problem (land ownership and speculative rent) and presents his solution (the Land Value Tax) in Volume II. He spends this entire second volume explaining why Land Value Tax is moral and just, how it should be applied, and why it will solve all our problems.

For the sake of the reader's attention span, I'll just cover the chapters that constitute the core of George's philosophy. All block quotes are from *Progress & Poverty* unless otherwise noted.

3

The Problem

George opens by observing an unkept promise made by Industrialists: "it was expected, that labor-saving inventions would lighten the toil and improve the condition of the laborer."

Industrialization should have freed humankind from drudgery and want. Instead, George sees:

> *complaints of industrial depression; of labor condemned to involuntary idleness; of capital massed and wasting; of pecuniary distress among business men; of want and suffering and anxiety among the working class...*

If we finally have the necessary material conditions and technology for utopia, why this suffering, waste, and inefficiency?

Also, why are there industrial depressions? How can there be periods where laborers desperately want to work but can't find employment at the very same time capital sits around in useless piles, begging to be put to productive use?

Contrary to popular explanations at the time, George argues it "can hardly be accounted for by local causes" such as military expenditures, tariffs, type of government, dense vs. sparse populations, or paper money vs. hard currency. This is because he sees the same basic problem everywhere no matter how different the countries themselves are. Behind these various troubles, George says there must lie a common cause.

Pulling no punches, the man lays the blame at the feet of *progress itself.*

> *that poverty and all its concomitants show themselves in communities just as they develop into the conditions toward which material progress tends - proves that the social difficulties existing wherever a certain stage of progress has been reached, do not arise from local circumstances, but are, in some way or another, engendered by progress itself...*

This is a pretty bold claim: namely, that the resilience of poverty, oppression, and inequality in the face of advancing economic development is not some embarrassing accident we'll eventually get around to fixing, but rather an inescapable consequence of our socioeconomic system.

A BRIEF INTERLUDE FROM THE FUTURE

It has been over 140 years since he wrote the book, so let's hop in my time machine and see how much of George's complaint is still relevant.

Back then, the United States was still in the throes of the Long Depression (Glasner, 1997), which according to the *shortest* estimate lasted from 1873 to 1879.

Below is a graph of the boom-bust business cycle going back to the 1870's—clearly, recessions were much more frequent and severe in George's time than they are today. The last three decades of the 19th century were wracked with so many panics and crises in quick succession that some historians count the Long Depression as lasting for a full 23 years from 1873 to 1896!

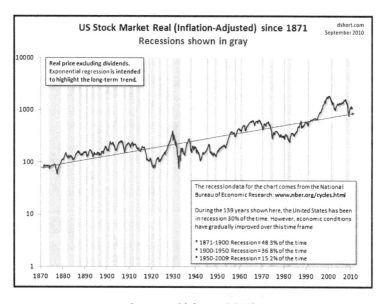

Source: (dshort, 2010)

After the Great Depression in the 1930's, we see a sharp decrease in the duration and frequency of recessions. They're still with us now (and the 2020 COVID recession was the worst since the Great Depression), but you'd still rather be living in modern times than in 1879. So, have we solved the problem? Is George's complaint obsolete? I mean, this graph of GDP per capita from Stephen Pinker's *Enlightenment*

Now suggests things are improving in many ways (Pinker, 2018):

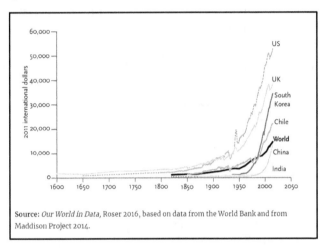

Source: *Our World in Data,* Roser 2016, based on data from the World Bank and from Maddison Project 2014.

Also, extreme poverty has been going down everywhere (Roser & Ortiz-Ospina, Global Extreme Poverty, 2013):

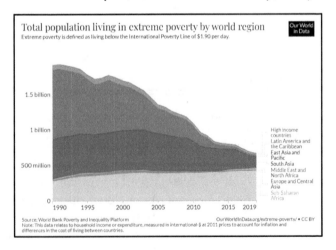

This can't be the entire picture, or nobody would be complaining about poverty and inequality.

This graph (Amoros, 2019) shows that as consumer goods have gotten cheaper in the United States, health care, higher education, child care, etc., have skyrocketed in price, as examined in great detail on Slate Star Codex (Alexander, Considerations on Cost Disease, 2017):

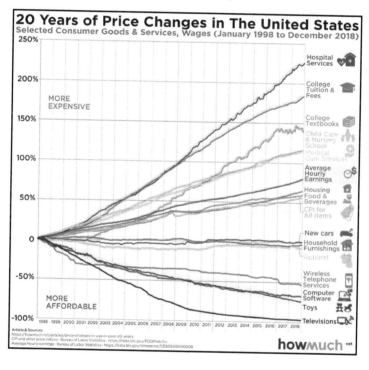

And what about Inequality? In the USA it seems to have reverted to levels not seen since the Great Depression, and even when it was at its lowest in 1978, the top 0.1% (not even the top 1%!) still enjoyed a massively disproportionate share of Wealth (Saez E. a., 2016):

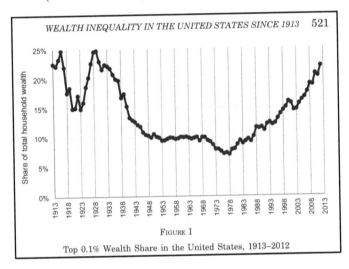

FIGURE I

Top 0.1% Wealth Share in the United States, 1913–2012

Also, The Rent Is Too Damn High (Woo, 2016):

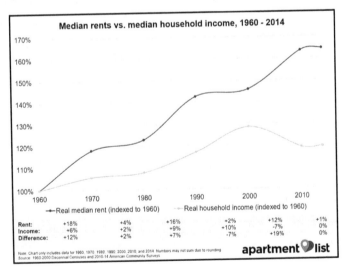

(Al, 2011):

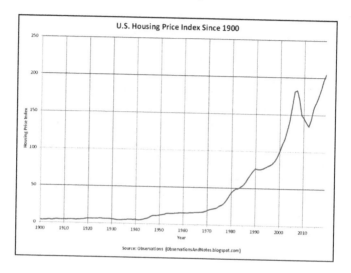

Although 2022 seems better than 1879 in absolute material terms, George's complaint still rings true: healthcare and higher education are increasingly unaffordable, inequality is as bad as it ever was, and The Rent Is Too Damn High.

Even if all of these measures had improved as well, we still have to contend with a fundamental complaint: how can human civilization have piled up nearly $400 trillion, an amount of wealth best described as absolutely *banana pants insane*, and yet still have poverty, oppression, and cyclical recessions (Credit Suisse, 2020)?

Yes, greed, evil, and human nature will always be with us, but isn't it weird that we haven't eliminated these economic problems the same way we've eliminated Smallpox, Scurvy, and having to write your scathing polemics about Thomas Jefferson by candlelight with a goose feather?

I now give the mic back to George, who closes the chapter with this haunting quote, first written 143 years ago:

> *If there is less deep poverty in San Francisco than in New York, is it not because San Francisco is yet behind New York in all that both cities are striving for? When San Francisco reaches the point where New York now is, who can doubt that there will also be ragged and barefooted children on her streets?*

I'll just leave this here (Associated Press, 2014):

> *SAN FRANCISCO (AP) — The number of homeless children in the U.S. has surged in recent years to an all-time high, amounting to one child in every 30, according to a comprehensive state-by-state report that blames the nation's high poverty rate, the lack of affordable housing and the impacts of pervasive domestic violence. ... The problem is particularly severe in California, which has one-eighth of the U.S. population but accounts for more than one-fifth of the homeless children with a tally of nearly 527,000.*

4

Wages and Capital

George insists sloppy terminology leads to sloppy thinking. Naturally, he spends an entire chapter beating words to death to correct this.

Let's start with "wealth."

WEALTH

The common usage, both then and now, is "anything with an exchange value." George doesn't like how this mixes dissimilar things.

By George, what is wealth?

Wealth is produced when nature's bounty is touched by human labor resulting in a tangible product that is the object of human desire.

Labor is required, but the amount and type doesn't matter—George offers the example of simply picking a berry off a bush as an act that transforms nature's gifts into human wealth. Note particularly that human desire is an important requirement of wealth; it doesn't matter how much work someone put into something, if it doesn't gratify human needs or desires in some way, it is not wealth.

Speaking of human desire, let's talk about "value."

Where does a thing's value come from? The prevailing theory of the day was the "labor theory of value" which originated with Adam Smith and David Ricardo, which says that labor is the source of value. The early formulations were a bit ambiguous. Here's Smith in *Wealth of Nations* for instance:

> *The value of any commodity . . . is equal to the quantity of labor which it enables him to purchase or command. Labor, therefore, is the real measure of the exchangeable value of all commodities.*

So . . . is a thing's value how much labor it takes to make the thing, or how much labor someone's willing to exchange for the thing?

Nowadays, labor theory of value is generally associated with Marx. Marx picks a lane and says the value of something is tied to the amount of "socially necessary labor" required to *produce* it.

George goes the other way (George, The Science of Political Economy, 1897):

> *It is never the amount of labor that has been exerted in bringing a thing into being that determines its value, but always the amount of labor that will be rendered in exchange for it.*

In other words, "a thing's value is whatever someone is willing to pay for it." This is in line with the so-called marginal revolution (the movement, not the blog[5]) and modern theories of value.

So that takes care of wealth. Now let's define labor, production, wages, capital, and land.

LABOR

Labor is the exertion of human beings. It is possible to labor to no avail (try punching a concrete wall), but typically humans labor towards an end, such as gaining wealth. But, whether or not we accomplish anything with our efforts, George calls them labor. Labor isn't just making things, by the way—it is also moving or exchanging them.

PRODUCTION

Production is labor applied "to the production of wealth." You know, productively. This is all human exertion that isn't punching a concrete wall and rewards you for your efforts with something that fits the definition of wealth. Said wealth is the "product of labor."

WAGES

George says, "whatever is received as the result or reward of exertion is 'wages.'"

No distinction here is made between blue-collar work and white-collar work—whether one is called "hourly pay" and the other is called "annual salary," George calls them both

---

[5] www.marginalrevolution.com

"wages." It doesn't matter whether you receive them from your boss, from customers, or from nature. If you do work and get something from it, you have received "wages."

With those basics under our belt, let's circle back to wealth—what are some examples?

By George, gold is wealth. Teddy bears are wealth. Tesla roadsters and candy canes and young adult vampire romance novels are wealth. The same goes for fish you've caught, deer you've hunted, and cool looking rocks you've picked up on your morning walk. The value of these things may differ, but if they're tangible, originate in nature, someone ever did a lick of work to make or acquire them, and a human being somewhere desires them for any reason, they're wealth.

It gets a little clearer when we ask what *isn't* wealth.

And by George, *money* isn't wealth.

Articles of gold are wealth because they're tangible things that have been dug up, crafted, and fulfill certain human desires. But paper currency, digital currencies, and other things that aren't inherently valuable but merely *represent* value are *not* wealth (outside of putting their physical articles in coin collections or making paper airplanes, and so forth). Now don't get the man wrong, these things are certainly *valuable*. They're just not *wealth*. They are certificates that represent *claims* on wealth. For any computer programmers in the audience, money is a *pointer* to wealth.

Likewise, stocks and bonds and other financial instruments are not wealth. These are also just claims on wealth. A creditor's title to debt isn't wealth either, it is just a claim on the debtor's (typically future) wealth. Writing not long after the Civil War, George points out that slaves are not wealth either, but represent "merely the power of one class to appropriate the earnings of another class."

Wealth, thus defined, is the terminal "ground truth" bits of the economy, and all the financial layers on top are fancy IOUs that just encode various claims on it.

George offers a thought experiment to test if something is wealth: if you produce a pile of gold, fish, or Lego bricks, you've clearly increased the amount of wealth in the world. But if you produce a giant pile of IOUs that just records who owns what and who owes what to whom, it doesn't matter how many of them you pile up or how long the chains of ownership get, you still haven't increased the amount of real wealth in the world.

Again, this isn't saying the IOUs aren't valuable, they are. However, they're only valuable because they ultimately point to real wealth. If you magically transported everyone over to a hypothetical Earth 2, carrying over all of Earth 1's money and financial instruments but none of Earth 1's tangible wealth, the value of all those IOUs would instantly evaporate.

Now, what about digital goods? Leaving things like Bitcoin aside for the moment, let's consider the case of a digital image file. Is such a thing wealth? By George, it is.

Digital though it may be, it is physically encoded on a storage device somewhere, and is thus tangible (it is not a purely abstract concept flitting about in Platonic heaven) and has its origins in nature. Human exertion built the computer that encodes it, and clicking the button that saves it to disk or displays it on your screen is labor (albeit a miniscule amount). Finally, it directly satisfies human desires (mine, at the very least). Its value may be negligible, but it is wealth.

By contrast, the digital bit sitting in some database that says I own a particular eBook or mp3 is just a digital IOU—a claim on the wealth that are the physical bits on my local storage device or remote server that digitally encodes the files. The fact that digital files don't *seem* particularly physical, and that they can be trivially and endlessly copied, doesn't mean that Henry George, magically transported to today, wouldn't regard them as wealth.

Okay, so is there anything else that's not wealth?

By George, Bitcoin isn't wealth, in case you were wondering. It is just a (very fancy) financial instrument, a digital claim on wealth. That also goes for most crypto assets—a token on some blockchain that says I own a painting by Banksy is just another IOU, regardless of the technical sophistication of its distributed trustless ledger.

What about intellectual property? Copyrights, patents, and trademarks are all different forms of *monopoly*—the exclusive, government-granted legal right to do a particular thing (publish a certain book, manufacture a certain product, use a certain name in business, etc.). The exclusive right to do or produce a thing, valuable as it may be, is not the thing itself. By George, monopoly is not wealth.

But there is something big that *is* wealth, the C-word.

CAPITAL

By George, capital is "wealth devoted to procuring more wealth" and it is the next thing he insists everyone is hopelessly confused about.

He quotes Adam Smith, agreeing with him thus far:

> *That part of a man's stock which he expects to afford him revenue is called his capital.*

He also gives us a short etymology lesson on the origin of the term:

> *The word capital, as philologists trace it, comes down to us from a time when wealth was estimated in cattle, and a man's income depended upon the number of head he could keep for their increase.*

("Per capita" being the Latin for "by head")

By George, all capital is wealth, but not all wealth is capital.

George notes capital is often described as being "stored up labor" and endorses this view—but what it really means, is capital is stored up *production.* It is not literally the *labor* that's stored up, but the *wealth* generated by it, set aside, and then dedicated to the purpose of getting more wealth.

George insists that it is the owner's *intention* that transforms wealth into capital. If you buy an old factory to throw parties in for your hipster friends, it is just wealth. But the minute you decide to put it to work to make something useful (or start charging your hipster friends a cover charge at the door) it becomes capital.

George therefore further insists that a laborer's daily bread and the clothes on their back do *not* count as capital, because a person must eat and wear clothes whether they work or not. The laborer's tools (and arguably their steel-toed work boots) can, however, be counted as capital because their purpose is to assist the laborer in getting more wealth by working for wages, and the laborer wouldn't acquire, use, and maintain those things otherwise.

George has more exclusions:

> *We must exclude from the category of capital everything that may be included either as land or labor.*

Human exertion (labor) by itself can never be capital. The *products* of human labor *become* capital when they are stored up and set to the purpose of getting more wealth. To muddle this distinction defeats the point of having separate terms for those things at all and prevents us from reasoning meaningfully about how they relate to one another. Labor is not capital, and neither is labor by itself wealth, it *produces wealth*—and if it ain't wealth, then it ain't capital.

That brings us to land.

LAND, LAND, LAND

By George, land is not wealth.

And it is *definitely* not capital.

The unique specialness of land is George's entire schtick and the very core of his philosophy.

The term land embraces, in short, all natural materials, forces, and opportunities.

That means that a field or a meadow is "land," as is a mountain. But so are the fish in the sea, the clouds in the sky, veins of gold in the earth's crust, and the oil deep underground. These things aren't yet wealth—not until human beings both a) desire them and b) touch them with labor.

So... land is not wealth.

But... how come? I mean, look: land is tangible, it "comes from nature," humans are always productively applying their labor to it, and it certainly seems capable of gratifying human desires.

George sees this reasoning as understandable, but insists it is the root mistake that leads other political economists astray—because for George, land just *is* nature itself.

Come again?

Land is the ultimate source of all wealth, but it is most useful to think of it as a *generator,* a completely separate entity from the wealth that human labor and desire draws from it.

Players of *Magic: The Gathering* and *Settlers of Catan* should already have a solid grasp of this distinction:

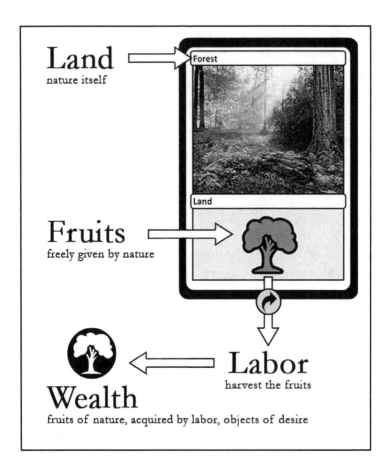

Land
nature itself

Forest

Land

Fruits
freely given by nature

Labor
harvest the fruits

Wealth
fruits of nature, acquired by labor, objects of desire

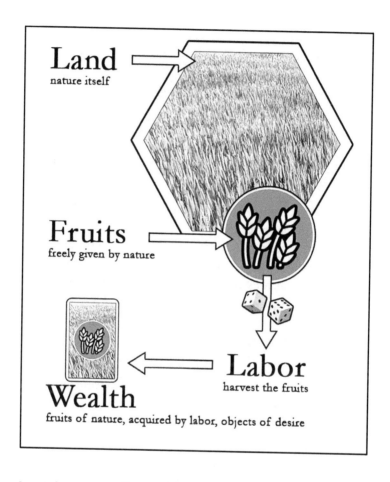

Land
nature itself

Fruits
freely given by nature

Labor
harvest the fruits

Wealth
fruits of nature, acquired by labor, objects of desire

In modern times, George would grant electromagnetic spectrum and orbital real estate for satellites the same status of "land" that already applies to farmland and terrestrial real estate. We don't even need to speculate about whether he'd attach this status to sunlight because he straight-up predicted solar power (George, Protection or Free Trade, 1886):

Even the lack of rain which makes some parts of the globe useless to man, may, if invention ever succeeds in directly utilizing the power of the sun's rays, be found to be especially advantageous for certain parts of production.

The important thing to grasp about land is that it comes before everything humans do or make, and is itself a thing no human can make.

Okay, smarty-pants, what about the Netherlands? They've been *making land* for centuries! Well, land in the Georgist sense doesn't refer simply to "dry land," but also the seabed, the oceans, and the skies above. The "new land" in the Netherlands counts as an *improvement* to land that already existed. The seabed was always there, but filling it in so that you can walk around on it makes it much more useful to human activity (George has a lot to say about improvements to land, which we'll get to later).

Okay, what is land *not*? "Nothing that is freely supplied by nature can be properly classed as capital."

By George, land is not wealth.
And since it is not wealth, it is not capital.

Okay, we get it. Land is very special to Mr. George and we must never put it in the same category as wealth, labor, capital, wages, production, money, or anything else. Why exactly is this so damn important?

Well, by George, if you treat land the same way you would a bar of pig iron, an hour of work, or a dollar bill, before you know it, you'll get poverty paradoxically advancing alongside progress, inexplicable bouts of industrial depression, literal genocides and holocausts (he's dead serious about this), and The Rent Being Too Damn High.

With terminology now firmly established, George moves on to the relationship between wages and capital.

3-FOR-1 SPECIAL ON WAGES, CAPITAL, AND LABOR

I'm condensing three chapters here because they all deal with the same basic thing. The question George wants to answer is: "Why, in spite of increase in productive power, do wages tend to a minimum which will give but a bare living?"

The conventional wisdom of George's time is that wages are governed by a fixed ratio between the number of laborers and the amount of capital devoted to their employment, because "the increase in the number of laborers tends naturally to follow and overtake any increase in capital."

Therefore, it doesn't matter how much capital you throw at employing workers, it'll just attract even more workers splitting it up, so although wages might temporarily wiggle a bit in the long term they'll always settle back to a "natural" minimum. (As we'll see in the next section, this argument stems from Malthusianism).

George spends some time methodically poking holes in the theory (its predictions don't line up with the facts he observes), and then sets out to prove his replacement theory:

> *wages, instead of being drawn from capital, are in reality drawn from the product of the labor for which they are paid. . .During the time [the*

> *laborer] is earning the wages he is advancing*
> *capital to his employer, but at no time, unless*
> *wages are paid before work is done, is the employer*
> *advancing capital to him.*

He starts by identifying the source of confusion:

> *Because wages are generally paid in money, and in*
> *many of the operations of production are paid*
> *before the product is fully completed, or can be*
> *utilized, it is inferred that wages are drawn from*
> *pre-existing capital. . .*

I mean, the old theory seems sensible: the employer has capital and uses it to pay wages. However you slice it, capital's investment gets paid back by production when it takes its cut, so does it even make a difference to talk about where wages are "drawn" from? Value goes out, value comes in, isn't it all a wash?

By George, it isn't: in the old theory, because capital "must come first," it follows that "industry is limited by capital— that capital must be accumulated before labor is employed," which leads to a reductio ad absurdum.

> *We are told that capital is stored-up or*
> *accumulated labor— "that part of wealth which is*
> *saved to assist future production." If we substitute*
> *for the word "capital" this definition of the word,*
> *the proposition carries its own refutation, for that*
> *labor cannot be employed until the results of labor*
> *are saved becomes too absurd for discussion.*

George anticipates the following rejoinder: well, when we say 'labor is paid out of capital' we don't mean it as an absolute statement for all stages of human development (or else we have a chicken-and-the-egg problem and civilization could never have begun), we just mean it applies to, say, every civilization that's left the stone age.

George will have none of it and spends three entire chapters relentlessly beating to death the idea that wages are drawn from capital instead of from production.

He starts with the simple case where wages are paid in the form of direct, concrete wealth, then moves on to the more complex case where people are paid in money and other instruments.

LABORING FOR WAGES

Imagine a fishing village where nobody cooperates—each person digs up their own worms to use as bait and catches their own fish. Then they discover labor specialization and realize they can catch more fish together if one specializes in digging and the other in catching. The digger digs, the catcher catches, and they share the fish. The digger really contributes as much to the catch as the one who physically pulls the fish off the hook even though the digger never directly "caught" a fish, and the fish he gets for his work is directly paid out of his contribution to the total production. Later, our fisherfolk invent canoes, and one stays home making and repairing canoes. This increases the haul of the digger and catcher, and the canoe maker gets paid out of her contribution to the increased production. This cycle deepens as society continues to advance. The work the specialist puts in causes more fish to be caught, and that person's wages is drawn from the growing pile of fish. As George puts it: "Earning is making."

George gives another example:

> *If I take a piece of leather and work it up into a pair of shoes, the shoes are my wages—the reward of my exertion. Surely they are not drawn from capital—either my capital or any one else's capital—but are brought into existence by the labor of which they become the wages; and in obtaining this pair of shoes as the wages of my labor, capital is not even momentarily lessened one iota... As my labor goes on, value is steadily added, until, when my labor results in the finished shoes, I have my capital plus the difference in value between the material and the shoes.*

And another:

> *If I hire a man to gather eggs, to pick berries, or to make shoes, paying him from the eggs, the berries, or the shoes that his labor secures, there can be no question that the source of the wages is the labor for which they are paid.*

George goes on to say it doesn't matter if you're paid in money or directly in wealth, because the money is a direct claim on the underlying wealth. It also doesn't matter if you get paid on commission. Imagine a whaling ship where each crewman gets paid a share out of whatever the ship catches. When the ship sails back into port with a hold full of whale oil and bone, the crew gets paid in money, the owner simultaneously adds to his capital oil and bone. The crew's money directly represents their share of the concrete wealth that is the oil and bone. The owner's capital hasn't decreased, and the workers drew their wages directly from the production.

Let's get to the point, Mr. George: wages aren't drawn from capital but instead from production. Great, let's grant that— *so what?*

George hammers away at this because thinking wages are drawn from capital leads to a false conclusion: that "labor cannot exert its productive power unless supplied by capital with maintenance."

"Maintenance?" Well, workers need food and clothing, and they get paid by their employers, so you could imagine capital as a limiting factor on labor. But by George, food and clothing isn't capital, it is just wealth, as we said before.

And with regard to wages, the point is that the employer always gets "paid" first, because the second the laborer produces value, the employer's capital increases:

> *As in the exchange of labor for wages the employer always gets the capital created by the labor before he pays out capital in the wages, at what point is his capital lessened even temporarily?*

Okay, but what if I'm just a terrible businessman and I pay somebody $500 an hour to smash Ming vases, then sell the fragments as aggregate to a construction crew for a few pennies a pound, all at a tremendous loss? Surely *then* the laborer's wages must be drawn from my capital, because there's not enough productive value generated by the labor to draw them from!

George says okay, sure, but only because I'm an idiot and will soon be out of business:

> *Yet, unless the new value created by the labor is less than the wages paid, which can be only an exceptional case, the capital which he had before in money he now has in goods—it has been changed in form, but not lessened.*

Fair enough, Mr. George, but what if I'm building some enormously expensive multi-decade project, like a dam or a nuclear power plant or a cathedral? The kind of thing we call a "capital-intensive" project? What do you have to say to that?

George points out that as laborers labor, they progressively add value to whatever they're producing. Take the case of a shipwright building ships for an employer—even if the boss can't sell a half-finished ship, it still holds value (for one, it costs less to finish a half-finished ship than no ship at all). With every stroke of the laborers' work, the employer who owns the shipyard gets an incremental increase in his stock of capital.

> *It is not the last blow, any more than the first blow, that creates the value of the finished product—the creation of value is continuous, it immediately results from the exertion of labor.*

A pedant would point out that the "last hit" that finishes the product adds disproportionate value, but George's point is just to establish that value is continuously created, and doesn't magically come into being all at once right at the end.

George further points out that if you look at things like agriculture you'll see the market directly acknowledging his theory:

> *As a plowed field will bring more than an*
> *unplowed field, or a field that has been sown more*
> *than one merely plowed... It is tangible in the case*
> *of orchards and vineyards which, though not yet in*
> *bearing, bring prices proportionate to their age.*

George freely admits that capital can be *required* for certain kinds of work, but he disagrees with what its purpose is. It's *not* a pool that wages get paid out of.

He goes on for another chapter on "The Maintenance of Laborers Not Drawn From Capital" but I think we can safely skip it and move on. To summarize, George hammers to absolute death the idea that Laborers derive their own maintenance (food/shelter/clothing/etc.) from their wages, with George insisting it is drawn from production and... you guessed it, *not from capital.*

At least some of George's ideas will not seem so radical to modern readers (especially those already critical of neoclassical economics), but it is important to understand that at the time, almost everything he was saying was considered deeply radical and shocking. Capital was the fundamental driving force of the economy and labor was utterly dependent on it, and the Malthusian theory of overpopulation was the accepted explanation for why wages were low and workers were starving (Malthusianism's core tenet is that human overpopulation inevitably leads to widespread poverty).

Political Cartoon literally demonizing Henry George
Puck magazine, Oct. 20, 1886

THE REAL FUNCTIONS OF CAPITAL

Okay, Mr. George. You've spent three whole chapters beating me over the head with what the functions of capital *aren't*. So, what *are* the functions of capital?

Capital "increases the power of labor to produce wealth."

How?

1. By enabling labor to apply itself more effectively (power tools are powerful)

2. By availing labor of the reproductive forces of nature (cows make baby cows)

3. By making possible the division & specialization of labor (you dig bait, I'll catch fish)

Capital is a *force multiplier* that supercharges the productive power of labor. It doesn't supply labor with raw materials (nature does), nor does it provide for the maintenance of workers (who eat bread by the sweat of their own brow).

George says this is why capital isn't a limit on industry.

...okay, George grants that capital may limit the *form* of industry. You can't plow without a plow or milk without a cow. George also grants that the lack of specialized tools *can* greatly limit productivity because you don't get the benefit of the force-multiplying effect of capital.

Um... aren't you contradicting yourself here, Mr. George? You spent all this time hammering home your doctrine of wages to prove that capital doesn't limit industry, but you just said its absence can limit both the form *and* the productivity of labor!

Time to unpack what we mean by "limit" and be super clear about it from now on:

> But to say that capital may limit the form of
> industry or the productiveness of industry is a very
> different thing from saying that capital limits
> industry.

Okay, what do you mean?

> For the dictum of the current political economy
> that "capital limits industry," means not that
> capital limits the form of labor or the

productiveness of labor, but that it limits the
exertion of labor.

Okay, I think I see what he's saying. The existing school of
thought says that *because* capital provides labor with both
materials and maintenance, *therefore* if capital dries up, labor
productivity must go down because workers will have nothing
to work on, and nothing to eat or wear. Labor is thus
"limited" by capital, for without it, it is literally and
metaphorically *starved* for capital.

But George says no—the only way capital actually "limits"
productivity in real life is in the degrees by which it force-
multiplies labor's productivity and unlocks certain forms of
labor in the tech tree. The kind of "limit" George objects to
is the idea that you need capital just to get any work done at
all, or that without capital to sustain it, labor will shrivel up.
Instead, capital is rocket fuel that labor supplies to itself by
investing a portion of its wages.

And yet, with all the awesome slots we've unlocked on the
tech tree, and barrels and barrels of rocket fuel to fire up
eager laborers, we still find our economy sinking into
mysterious depressions. *Something* is gumming up the works,
but it is not a simple scarcity of capital: "The real limitation is
not the want of capital, but the want of its proper
distribution."

Or as G.K. Chesterton said, "Too much capitalism does not
mean too many capitalists, but too few capitalists"
(Chesterton, 1920). This might seem like a pedantic
distinction—misallocated capital could be said to be "scarce"

capital—but they're not the same thing at all. As Francis Bacon said in 1625 (Quote Investigator, 2016):

> *Riches were like [Manure]: When it lay, upon an heape, it gave but a stench, and ill odour; but when it was spread upon the ground, then it was cause of much fruit.*

Because the prevailing theories of George's time are based on incorrect ideas about the relation between wages and capital, "all remedies, whether proposed by professors of political economy or workingmen, which look to the alleviation of poverty either by the increase of capital or the restriction of the number of laborers or the efficiency of their work, must be condemned."

In short, more investment, more protectionism, and more efficiency programs can't, won't, and haven't fixed poverty and industrial depressions because they all proceed from false premises.

Having finally beaten the nexus of wages, capital, and labor into a bloody pulp, George turns his eyes towards another leading theory for why everything is terrible: the specter of overpopulation.

5

Population and Subsistence

The entire second book of *Progress and Poverty* might as well be titled "Why Malthus is Dumb and Wrong and Bad."

It is a thorough critique of Malthusianism, a philosophy attributed to English cleric Thomas Malthus, which ascribes economic crises to the exponential growth of the human population, which must necessarily end in catastrophe: "according to Malthusian theory, poverty appears as increase in population necessitates the more minute division of subsistence."

THE MORAL CASE AGAINST MALTHUS

George attacks Malthusian ideas not just because they're wrong, but because they make it easier to accept the prevailing theory of wages (as more capital is allocated, laborers will keep popping up like weeds to gobble it up, so wages must eternally stagnate). George draws a straight line between these faulty ideas and holocausts and genocides—specifically citing how colonial oppression in China, India, and Ireland were explicitly justified on Malthusian grounds.

One million people died in the English-engineered Irish potato famine alone, and when you add in those who fled, the entire population declined by *25% percent* (Dorney, 2016). This isn't a tenuous link either—George directly connects the completely avoidable famine to his favorite bugbear, private landownership and extortionate rent.

Malthusianism in George's time was wildly popular, and often invoked by the ascendant proponents of Social Darwinism, who took Charles Darwin's theory of "survival of the fittest" and recast it as a moral justification for the "Just World Hypothesis." Essentially, those that are doing well do so because they are more "fit," and those that are less "fit" tend to perish, and furthermore, this brutal process will actively "improve" the human race. This philosophy was the energizing intellectual force behind both the Eugenics movement and Nazi Germany.

George clearly hates everything about this philosophy but engages with the most charitable interpretation of it anyways:

> *The Malthusian doctrine, as at present held, may be thus stated in its strongest and least objectionable form:*
>
> *That population, constantly tending to increase, must, when unrestrained, ultimately press against the limits of subsistence, not as against a fixed, but as against an elastic barrier, which makes the procurement of subsistence progressively more and more difficult. And thus, wherever reproduction has had time to assert its power, and is unchecked by prudence, there must exist that degree of want which will keep population within the bounds of subsistence.*

The weak form of Malthusianism is "people are as dumb as deer and will breed endlessly until there's not enough food and everyone starves to death."

The strong form of Malthusianism is, "of course people aren't mindless deer charging into a brick wall, but there is a firm upper limit that can only give so much before nature will cull the herd without mercy."

And by George, we can't just dismiss the strong form out of hand: "what seems clearer than that there are too many people?"

However, George is suspicious of how easily the Malthusian theory justifies contemporary economic assumptions and assuages the moral sensibilities of the establishment:

> *The great cause of the triumph of this theory is that, instead of menacing any vested right or antagonizing any powerful interest, it is eminently soothing and reassuring to the classes who, wielding the power of wealth, largely dominate thought... It furnishes a philosophy by which Dives as he feasts can shut out the image of Lazarus who faints with hunger at his door;*

He points out how it lets self-styled "Good Christian Men" reframe their own greed and indifference as just plain good sense:

> *In this view, he who in the midst of want has accumulated wealth, has but fenced in a little oasis from the driving sand which else would have overwhelmed it. He has gained for himself, but has*

hurt nobody. And even if the rich were literally to obey the injunctions of Christ and divide their wealth among the poor, nothing would be gained.

(Aside: I've sadly heard this *exact* defense offered by many of my fellow Christians.)

Okay, George makes a strong *moral* case against Malthusianism. However, a moral case isn't enough, and I think this is where many activists of all political stripes go wrong. If you attack the premises of an idea as "dangerous" because it could lead to bad consequences, you're still stuck with a real problem if the premises that animate that "dangerous" idea turn out to be *actually true.* If they're true, we're stuck with them, and unless your competing policy admits to the same grim facts, your opponent will just dismiss your entire argument and more importantly, so will their audience.

But if the premises *aren't true,* then the dangerous and scary policy prescription—say, "let the Irish starve to death"—is both evil *and* unnecessary. History has shown that many officials will shrug their shoulders at "evil" policies so long as they believe them to be "necessary" (The New York Times, 1968):

Major Describes Move

BENTRE, Feb. 7 (AP)—"It became necessary to destroy the town to save it," a United States major said today.

He was talking about the decision by allied commanders to bomb and shell the town regardless of civilian casualties, to rout the Vietcong.

Having established that Malthusianism is bad, let's further establish that it is *false*.

A BRIEF INTERLUDE FROM THE FUTURE

From where we're sitting in 2022, we don't even need George to refute Malthusianism, history has done that for us.

Instead of increasing at an exponential rate, fertility rates are crashing all over the world (Roser, Fertility Rate, 2017). Not in one country, but in virtually every country, and in many the birth rate is already below replacement. Fertility rates have been crashing so hard that some are calling it a "Global Fertility Crisis" (Gallagher, 2020). The absolute size of the human population is still growing, but this is just due to inertia; the human population will peak somewhere between 9 and 10 billion in the 2060's, and then decline from there (Roser, Future Population Growth, 2019).

Malthus failed to anticipate two crucial things:

1. Advances in food production technology like the Green Revolution, a period of major advancement in agricultural technology throughout the world beginning in the late 1960's that vastly increased crop yields worldwide.

2. That humans can control their own fertility rates.

Okay, back to the 19th century.

THE ECONOMIC CASE AGAINST MALTHUS

George's strongest arguments against Malthusianism strike directly at the *provably false* claims of its 19th century proponents and provide some extremely salient applications of George's philosophy.

George takes up the cause of India, China, and Ireland, which were often cited as examples of "overpopulated" countries where many have starved and been forced to emigrate. Per the Malthusians, this is the fault of too many of these poor, ignorant, and deficient people crammed together in too small a space.

By George, it couldn't be the fault of population density—in his time, Germany, Belgium, England, the Netherlands and Italy all had *higher* population densities than India, China, and Ireland, and could therefore support higher populations with the right conditions. And there was certainly nothing wrong with the people themselves:

> *This arises from no innate deficiency in the people,*
> *for the Hindoo, as comparative philology has*
> *shown, is of our own blood, and China possessed a*
> *high degree of civilization and the rudiments of the*
> *most important modern inventions when our*
> *ancestors were wandering savages.*

Instead:

> *It arises from the form which the social*
> *organization has in both countries taken, which has*
> *shackled productive power and robbed industry of*
> *its reward.*

India was poor not because it had too many Indians, but because it was oppressed by too many Englishmen:

> *The millions of India have bowed their necks*
> *beneath the yokes of many conquerors, but worst*
> *of all is the steady grinding weight of English*
> *domination... India now is like a great estate owned*
> *by an absentee and alien landlord*

George gives us lots of details about the plight of India, China, and Ireland, but for the sake of brevity I'm just going to present the heartbreaking case of the Great Irish Potato Famine and let it stand in for all three.

To sum up, from 1845 to 1852 there was a period of mass starvation and disease in Ireland. About one *million* people died, and another million fled the country. The entire population dropped by about 25% (Dorney, 2016):

> *The extreme poverty of the peasantry and the low rate of wages there prevailing, the Irish famine, and Irish emigration, are constantly referred to as a demonstration of the Malthusian theory worked out under the eyes of the civilized world.*

Many prominent intellectuals of the day looked at the crisis, shook their heads, and said—what do you expect when those ignorant Irish Catholics breed like rabbits and strain Ireland's carrying capacity to its limit? It's just natural selection at work! George will have none of it:

> *The laborer was just as effectually stripped by as merciless a horde of landlords, among whom the soil had been divided as their absolute possession, regardless of any rights of those who lived upon it.*

Okay, they had to pay some rent, so what? Didn't they bring their suffering on themselves? Why, the intellectuals ask, didn't the Irish work harder, why did they not improve their local economy and agricultural base? And most importantly, why did they depend on a single monoculture crop (the potato) if a single blight could knock out their entire food supply? By George, because *The Rent Was Too Damn High!*

> *Tenants... even if the rack-rents which they were forced to pay had permitted them, did not dare to make improvements which would have been but the signal for an increase of rent. Labor was thus applied in the most inefficient and wasteful manner.*

The Irish were really trapped. Working harder to improve the farmland to increase its yield could actually leave them *worse* off. Any increase in their land's productivity goes to the

landlord in the form of increased rents. But even this
structural impoverishment of the land wasn't sufficient to
cause the famine. Ireland still produced enough food to feed
its people:

> *For when her population was at its highest, Ireland*
> *was a food-exporting country. Even during the*
> *famine, grain and meat and butter and cheese were*
> *carted for exportation along roads lined with the*
> *starving and past trenches in which the dead were*
> *piled.*

People were literally starving to death, but because of the
structure of land ownership, they couldn't even pay their rent,
let alone purchase the food grown from their own lands and
raised with their own hands. Since the local population
couldn't afford it, the (English) landlords sold it abroad to the
highest bidder.

> *It went not as an exchange, but as a tribute—to*
> *pay the rent of absentee landlords; a levy wrung*
> *from producers by those who in no wise*
> *contributed to production... they lived on the*
> *potato, because rack-rents stripped everything else*
> *from them.*

The Rent Is Too Damn High, and it is not because those who
are designated as the underclass of the day are having too
many babies or are too uneducated, too ignorant, too
superstitious, too religious, too lazy, or too foreign.

George gets *really* mad about this and calls out John Stuart
Mill and Henry Thomas Buckle by name for lending credence
to the Malthusian explanation of Ireland's suffering.

*I know of nothing better calculated to make the
blood boil than the cold accounts of the grasping,
grinding tyranny to which the Irish people have
been subjected, and to which, and not to any
inability of the land to support its population, Irish
pauperism and Irish famine are to be attributed;
and were it not for the enervating effect which the
history of the world proves to be everywhere the
result of abject poverty, it would be difficult to
resist something like a feeling of contempt for a
race who, stung by such wrongs, have only
occasionally murdered a landlord!*

Now that George has spent an entire book yelling at
Malthus, we can finally move on to the meat of his
philosophy—the "laws of distribution" that govern the
economic universe and control how different people get
rewarded by the economy.

6

The Laws of Distribution

When society produces wealth, who gets different shares of it, and why? Let's start by beating some words to death.

By George, we're told that there are three factors in production: *Land, Labor,* and *Capital.* For each of these terms there must be a "law of distribution" that explains how each gets compensated for its part in production.

The reward you get from production by owning *Land* is called *Rent.*

The reward you get from production by supplying *Labor* is called *Wages.*

The reward you get from production by supplying *Capital* is called ... um, what?

We're looking for a term that clearly expresses the return to capital alone and *nothing* else.

The closest thing we have is *Interest,* and that's probably good enough.

George gives the common definition of interest as "the return for the use of capital, exclusive of any labor in its use or management, and exclusive of any risk, except such as may be involved in the security." This is pretty close to what we want—something that expresses the *sole* return to capital without mixing in anything else.

But ... what about *Profits?*

Profits is "almost synonymous" with *revenue,* assuming you have some left after you deduct expenses. It means a gain in money or wealth, but the trouble is this gain is a mix of *rent, wages,* and "compensations for the risk peculiar to the various uses of capital." What we want is a term that means the return to capital *alone,* totally separate from the return to laborers and landowners. As George puts it, "To talk about the distribution of wealth into rent, wages, and profits is like talking of the division of mankind into men, women, and human beings."

Before he presents his model for how it all works, George spends a few pages talking about how everyone from Adam Smith on down got confused about this (spoiler: it is tied up with thinking wages are drawn from capital).

THE CONVENTIONAL (AND MOSTLY WRONG) LAWS OF DISTRIBUTION IN GEORGE'S TIME

CONVENTIONAL LAW 1: *Wages* are determined by the amount of capital devoted to the payment and subsistence of labor, divided up by the number of laborers.

CONVENTIONAL LAW 2: *Rent* is determined by something called the "margin of production," AKA the "margin of cultivation."

This is the only conventional law of distribution that George accepts as correct, and we'll explain it in detail (with pictures!) below.

CONVENTIONAL LAW 3: *Interest* is the ratio between capital demanded by borrowers and supplied by lenders, falling as wages rise and vice versa. To quote Mill, interest is determined "by the cost of labor to the capitalist."

The problem is if Land, Labor, and Capital are the only three factors of production, and each gets its own return, then the three returns should balance. In other words:

Return to Production = Rent + Wages + Interest

If your three returns sum to more or less than 100% of the return to production, something's off, and George says the old laws don't add up—the only one of these he accepts is the law of rent. What's wrong with the other two?

Firstly, we've got to stop using "profits" to mean a return to capital. If we look into a profit stream, we see more than one kind of thing. Conventional economists list the following:

1.   Wages of "superintendence"

2.   Compensation for risk

3.   Return for the use of capital

"Superintendence" is a fancy word for management. White-collar though it may be, it is still labor, and its compensation is *wages*. That's not a return to capital.

As for compensation for risk, George says that risk averages out and disappears when you take the God's eye view and sum all of society's transactions together. If I take the winning side of a bet and you take the losing side, I enjoy gain, you suffer loss, but the amount of wealth in the world hasn't actually increased as a result of our bet.

That leaves return for the use of capital, which George calls *interest:*

> *I shall therefore, consistently with the definitions of political economists, use the term interest as signifying that part of the produce which goes to capital.*

Okay, great, so now we're clear on what the laws of distribution *aren't,* can George tell us what they *are?*

GEORGE'S LAWS OF DISTRIBUTION

LAND is "all natural opportunities or forces" and its return is RENT.

LABOR is "all human exertion" and its return is WAGES.

CAPITAL is "all wealth used to produce more wealth" and its return is INTEREST.

George says the false assumption at the root of the old theories is in thinking of "capital as the prime factor in production, land as its instrument, and labor as its agent or tool."

George makes the following assertions:

1. "Labor can be exerted only upon land"

2. "It is from land that the matter which it transmutes into wealth must be drawn"

3. "Capital is not a necessary factor in production"

Therefore, we should always put land first in all our inquiries rather than capital, which ought to come last.

George then sets out his three laws of distribution.

THE LAW OF RENT

Let's be careful about the word "Rent." In modern usage, there is the concept of "Economic Rent" as well as "Rent" in the everyday sense of regular payments you make in exchange for the use of something that you are "renting." The modern definition of "Economic Rent," per the Encyclopaedia Britannica is:

> *[Economic] Rent is represented as the difference between the total return to a factor of production (land, labour, or capital) and its supply price—that is, the minimum amount necessary to attain its services.*

To be clear, Economic Rent is a bad thing—all taking, no giving. When George uses the word "Rent," he specifically means the return to land, and this is what he says it is: "Rent, in short, is the share in the wealth produced which the exclusive right to the use of natural capabilities gives to the owner."

Land has zero cost of production because it is already there and you can't make it. This means that any payment or benefit you can realize by excluding others from using land (or its fruits) is necessarily "in excess of the costs needed to bring that factor into production."

By George, all land rent is Economic Rent.

Furthermore, any piece of land has only one seller, and no producers. This further meets the definition of Monopoly—Greek for "one seller." This is why you hear Georgists talking about "land monopoly."

Land has value because people are willing to pay you for the privilege of using it. The price of rent derives from the most marginal land available.

I'll explain with an example. Let's grade some imaginary lots according to their productivity by using abstract utility points, or "utils."

Lot A is good fertile land worth 100 utils.
Lot B is just as good, also worth 100 utils.
Lot C is marginal land worth 10 utils.

Let's say I own Lot A. If Lot B is freely available to anyone to use, then I won't be able to charge you any rent on Lot A.

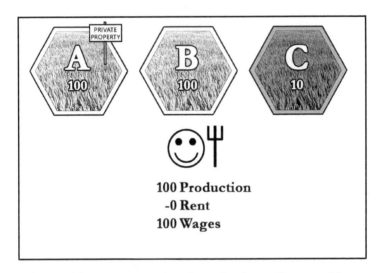

Why would you pay even 1 util worth of rent if you could just work on Lot B, earn 100 utils, and keep it all?

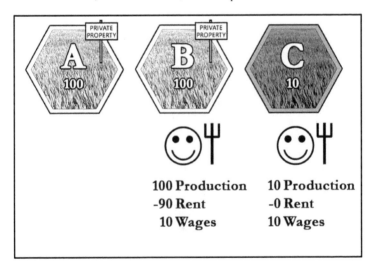

Once I buy Lot B, now you must pay me if you want to access 100-util land. How much can I charge? Well, you could always work on Lot C for free, yielding 10 utils. That means that I can charge at most 90 utils (100 - 90 = 10).

Here's the Law of Rent: rent is determined by the "margin of production" (AKA the "margin of cultivation")—the difference between how much you can produce from a particular piece of land (Lot A or B) compared to the most productive free alternative (Lot C).

Notice that I as the landlord am not really doing anything here other than owning the land, and yet I can extract a huge amount of value, because unlike capital, land is a hard limit on labor—you can't work without a place to work or without material that comes from nature. I take my share first without really contributing anything to production other than gatekeeping access to land.

> *Rent, in short, is the price of monopoly, arising from the reduction to individual ownership of natural elements which human exertion can neither produce nor increase.*

C'mon, is land really such a big deal?

In the popular imagination we pit "capitalists" against "laborers" but a lot of those "capitalists" are landowners in disguise, because in non-Georgist frameworks land is typically considered a kind of capital. George says landowners oppress both labor *and* capital, cheating both hard work and investment out of their fair share.

Okay, but is this still relevant in the modern age, with the internet and work-from-home? Obsessing about land just feels so "19th century." On the other hand, in Silicon Valley rents are famously off the charts, and those and all other rents seep into the economy at every level.

Workers priced out of living close by have to spend more time and money commuting longer distances to work, and businesses must devote an increasingly larger share of their production to landowners who aren't actively contributing anything to productivity. What else could explain why a family of four with an income of $100,000 in San Francisco is now considered to be living below the poverty line? (Poverty in San Francisco | City Performance Scorecards, 2022)

Here, take a look at this chart (Blanco, Bauluz, & Martínez-Toledano, 2018):

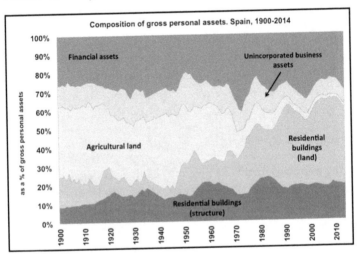

I found this in a tweet by Thomas Piketty[6], and it shows the breakdown of personal assets in Spain over the last 100+ years. The bulk of the value of personal assets is from landownership. This is still the case even though the chart includes "financial assets"—which are just IOUs that ultimately have something real (e.g. land or wealth) underpinning their value. If we exclude those, the true portion of overall value represented by land is even higher than this graph first implies.

And this isn't just Spain. Here's a graph Nate Blair made for the UK, excluding all financial instruments and only looking at real assets:

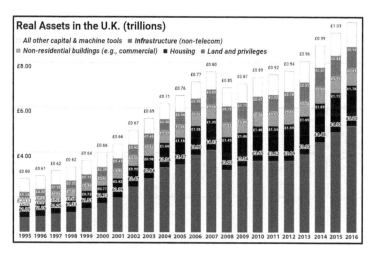

Based on data from the United Kingdom National Accounts: The Blue Book 2017. Published Oct 31, 2017. Revision Period: Beginning of each time series. Date of next release: July 2018. The "privileges" in "Land and

---

[6]https://twitter.com/PikettyLeMonde/status/963093728150933505

privileges" are things like taxi medallions[7] and patents, that were worth "almost zero" according to Nate.

No matter how hard you try, "there is no occupation in which labor and capital can engage which does not require the use of land." Whenever anyone does labor, the owner of some piece of land—whether it is the farm in the middle of Kansas that grows your food, the lot hosting the server farm sending bytes to your computing device, or the ground presently beneath your feet—is sticking their finger in the pie.

George reminds us that labor and capital will have to share whatever is left after landowners take off the top of production in rent:

> *As Produce = Rent + Wages + Interest,*
> *Therefore, Produce - Rent = Wages + Interest*

What happens when the productivity of land goes up?

Let's go back to Lot A and Lot B, both 100-util fields. Let's say they belong to different landlords, and I'm a tenant on Lot B. I improve the soil of the field I'm working on so now it is worth 110 utils. What happens?

My landlord raises the rent, of course!

---

[7] An artificially scarce set of transferable permits to operate a taxicab.

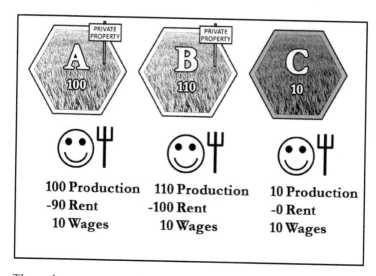

The only way wages (the return to labor) and interest (the return to capital) can go up as productivity increases is if land values fail to rise at the same rate.

THE LAW OF INTEREST

George wants to find the fundamental reason capital is able to produce wealth and justly claim a fair share of production.

Remember that capital is wealth devoted to getting more wealth. Since capital is wealth that begets wealth, it makes sense that if I lend it out to you, I miss out on the potential for it to grow while it is out of my hands. George says I am justly entitled to ask for more back than I originally gave you.

Let's say I loan you some corn seeds for a season. Had I not lent them to you, in a season's time I could have grown my own crop of corn and been left with more seed than I started with. So, in a perfectly square deal, you would need to give me back what I would have started with *and* what I should have expected to gain from natural increase (minus the value of the labor required to get things started).

Likewise with any other article of capital—say bricks or lumber. In the time I've spent without it while it was in your possession, I could have found someone else who had a better use for it than I did and exchanged it for something of theirs that I had a better use for, leaving me with capital of greater value. George says the act of progressively exchanging things in a way that increases subjective value for all involved is analogous to the natural forces of nature that make living capital (like corn and cows) grow over time.

Remember, "subjective value" is *real value*. In a game of *Settlers of Catan*, if I have two bricks and you have two lumber, neither of us can build anything. This is because a road costs one brick and one lumber, and neither of us has the correct set of resources. The simple act of trading one brick for one lumber means *both* of us are better off because each of us can now build a road. The quantity of bricks and lumber in the world didn't increase, but the quantity of *roads* (or potential roads) did, and that represents a real increase in wealth.

Interest thus springs from the "reproductive" powers of capital, whether that's biological reproduction, or the more abstract reproductive force of exchanging things so that you have a more valuable distribution of capital than you started with.

As to how it relates to the other two returns to production, the more powerful the "power of increase" the capital has, the greater return interest can claim compared to wages. If you're ploughing a field and I lend you a tractor which makes you ten times as productive, I can justly claim more compensation for that than if I lend you a mule that only makes you twice as productive. However, rent still holds the whip hand, so the margin of cultivation determines how much return is left over to divvy up between interest and wages.

This is because the net "reproductive" value of capital goes down given that rent is a general tax on overall productivity. The amount I would have gained by using the thing productively over the period of time it was out on loan (the amount I can justly charge in interest) is reduced by how much I have to pay in rent.

THE LAW OF WAGES

Wages, like interest, are limited by the margin of production. Within that limit there's not much to understand about how wages work except that people seek to satisfy their desires "with the least exertion," which is a fancy way of saying people don't like to get ripped off. If two bosses offer the same exact job, but one offers higher pay, I'm taking that gig. If two bosses pay the same, but one is asking for twice as much work, I'll tell that boss where he can stick it.

> *Wages depend upon the margin of production, or upon the produce which labor can obtain at the highest point of natural productiveness open to it without the payment of rent.*

With all three laws established George sums it up like so:

Where land is free and labor is unassisted by capital, the whole produce will go to labor as wages.

Where land is free and labor is assisted by capital, wages will consist of the whole produce, less that part necessary to induce the storing up of labor as capital.

Where land is subject to ownership and rent arises, wages will be fixed by what labor could secure from the highest natural opportunities open to it without the payment of rent.

Where natural opportunities are all monopolized, wages may be forced by the competition among laborers to the minimum at which laborers will consent to reproduce.

This is the reason George says that wages are so high in "new countries" where there's more land available than in countries where it has been locked up for centuries.

Here's how it all fits together:

Though neither wages nor interest anywhere increase as material progress goes on, yet the invariable accompaniment and mark of material progress is the increase of rent—the rise of land values.

And: "where the value of land is highest, civilization exhibits the greatest luxury side by side with the most piteous destitution."

7

How Progress Affects Wealth Distribution

As a society undergoes material progress, the rent goes up. Why? Let's break it down. Three things contribute to material progress:

1. Increasing population

2. Technological advance

3. Improvements in the social fabric

"Social fabric" is my term; George calls it "greater knowledge, education, government, police, manners, and morals, so far as they increase the power of producing wealth."

How does Population growth affect the distribution of wealth? Generally speaking, as you get more people your productivity grows exponentially rather than linearly: "The labor of 100 men. . .will produce much more than one hundred times as much as the labor of one man."

That's thanks to specialization and division of labor. This happens even in the absence of any technological advance. And as labor's productivity goes up, it makes it worth developing on more marginal (ie, less productive) lands, pushing the margin of production down (and outward geographically), which gives landlords more room to jack up rents.

A bustling town is a more valuable and productive place to live than a tiny hut in the middle of a remote forest. In the town there's a butcher, a baker, a candlestick maker, and others to supply you with whatever your heart desires. In the middle of the forest you have to do everything yourself, regardless of how abundant the natural resources might be. Every neighbor that moves in to town makes you "richer" in this sense because they contribute to the total productive potential of your community.

Population increase also drives productivity by making things valuable that were useless before. Let's say there's some resource on some land, say iron ore. Even if you have all the technology to mine and smelt it, you probably aren't capable of doing this whole operation yourself, and if nobody else lives there, you don't have anybody to sell the iron to. It's the presence of a civilization that will give that ore its value, and for that you need to increase the population. Until population shows up to give it value, the ore is "latent potential" in the land.

By George, increasing population increases the share of rent (and decreases the share of interest and wages) in two ways:

1.   It lowers the margin of production

2.   It brings out the latent potential of land

So that's it for population growth. Next, how does technological advance affect the distribution of wealth? Tech saves labor. It lets you accomplish the same thing with less work, or more things with the same amount of work. This leads to more wealth being produced. Now, what do you *need* to produce more things? Capital is nice to have, but the two things you *must* have are labor, and land. Wanting to make more things means more demand for land, because you can't labor without it. Further, when you reach the productive limit of the land available to you, you seek out more marginal lands, extending the margin of production. Demand for land goes up, land values go up, and soon enough *The Rent Is Too Damn High.*

This means that as you introduce advanced machines, the extra productivity they bring gets soaked up in rising land values, which gets extorted as rent.

> *Every labor-saving invention, whether it be a steam plow, a telegraph, an improved process of smelting ores, a perfecting printing press, or a sewing machine, has a tendency to increase rent.*

As a historical aside, I'll point out an extreme example of this: the cotton gin. This device massively decreased the amount of labor required to process cotton, which ironically *increased* the spread of slavery (Schur, 2005). Slaves are laborers who are compelled to pay all their wages in rent, and as the amount of slave labor required to process a unit of cotton went down, the margin of production was extended to more marginal lands. This caused the rents on the best lands to go up, further enriching slave-owning plantation landowners and increasing their influence. With the margin extended, demand shot up for land previously deemed unsuitable for cotton production, increasing the pressure to admit new states to the union as slave states. The gin's effect on entrenching slavery was so profound that it is commonly blamed for prolonging the institution and laying the foundations for the Civil War.

So that's how technological advance contributes to material advance and rising rents. Next, how does improved "social fabric" affect the distribution of wealth?

Improvements to the social fabric that just make society generically better do the same thing as population growth and technological advance. If the people in a neighborhood are nicer and more helpful, provide a robust network of mutual aid, start a bowling league and book club, etc., land values rise. That's because it is more desirable and productive to live in a place where you can e.g., trust your neighbor to watch your kid for an hour while also teaching them to whittle. Land value goes up, and so does the rent.

Now, let's talk about the *expectations* raised by material progress. What happens when people *know* something will increase in value?

That's right, they buy it up in a speculative frenzy and hold on to it forever, further driving the price up. With conventional speculative instruments like beanie babies or tulips, the bubble eventually pops. But land has unique properties that allow this vicious cycle to continue indefinitely.

What happens when a city is growing, technology is advancing, improvements are being made to land, and so forth? Land values go up. Sure, speculators can still lose their shirts if a city falls into decline, but this isn't nearly as hard to predict as volatility in penny stocks or what next year's hot Christmas toy will be.

As soon as there's a whiff of progress in a given area everyone starts buying and holding land, but not to use it themselves. In fact, speculators often keep it *out* of use, because this forces people to use less valuable land instead, pushing the margin of production down even *further*, forcing land values up, and now The Rent Is Too Damn High.

A Georgist pundit who goes by the online handle "geoliberal" explains the mindset of a speculator:

> The only thing investors actually maximize is risk adjusted rate of return. When you know rents will increase, your best return comes from buying extra land, not improving the land you have.

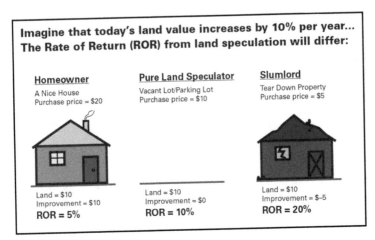

Illustration courtesy of geoliberal

This is how it is possible to have urban blight and slums in areas with extremely high land values. Even if there's a temporary dip in prices, speculators know that if they just keep holding, the general trend—absent a local collapse—is that land value always goes up.

Here's George:

> *Take now... some hard-headed business man, who has no theories, but knows how to make money. Say to him: "Here is a little village; in ten years it will be a great city—in ten years the railroad will have taken the place of the stage coach, the electric light of the candle; it will abound with all the machinery and improvements that so enormously multiply the effective power of labor. Will in ten years, interest be any higher?" He will tell you, "No!" "Will the wages of the common labor be any higher...?" He will tell you, "No the wages of*

common labor will not be any higher..." "What,
then, will be higher?" "Rent, the value of land. Go,
get yourself a piece of ground, and hold
possession."

...without doing one stroke of work, without
adding one iota of wealth to the community, in ten
years you will be rich! In the new city you may
have a luxurious mansion, but among its public
buildings will be an almshouse.

I don't think it is a coincidence that real estate is one of the
oldest investments on Earth and the principal concern of
basically every war ever.

8

The Problem Solved

We had two questions at the beginning of this book. The first was: "why are there industrial depressions?" And the second was: "why does poverty generally advance alongside of progress?"

The answer, according to Henry George, has to do with the questions of land and rent. To begin with the first: By George, industrial depressions are caused by *land speculation*.

Speculation tends to press the margin of production down until it is just past its limit, forcing labor and capital to accept returns so small that it actually hinders production or ceases altogether.

The saving grace is that as long as the population is growing and/or technology is improving, productivity will go up, and production will start again. But soon enough the land values go up. This drives speculators bidding up the price of land, anticipating future, even higher land values, which stresses the productive margin again.

This creates a cycle—productivity rises, economy booms, land values rise, production stagnates or stops. No matter how complicated or sophisticated the economy gets with layer upon layer of financialization and abstraction, when you unravel it all, George says this is the ultimate cause.

*Periods of industrial activity always culminate in a
speculative advance of land values, followed by
symptoms of checked production.*

This is how you get the baffling situation where able hands
are eager and willing to work, capital is ready to employ
them, natural materials are abundant, and yet the laborers are
idle and the factories stand empty.

That's it for industrial depressions. What about the other
paradox of poverty advancing alongside progress? By George,
poverty advances alongside progress because of *rent*.

*The reason why, in spite of increase of productive
power, wages constantly tend to a minimum which
will give but a bare living, is that, with increase in
productive power, rent tends to even greater
increase, thus producing a constant tendency to the
forcing down of wages.*

George backs this up with several pages of specific regional
figures demonstrating how land values have continued to
explode all over the world.

By George, on average and in the long run, no amount of
hard work from labor, no force multiplication from capital, no
increased gain from co-operation and specialization, no labor-
saving invention or increase in personal efficiency, work ethic,
or morals, can escape the long reach of rent.

*In short, increased power of production has
everywhere added to the value of land; nowhere has
it added to the value of labor;*

George notes that the mass die-off of the Black Death in England in the 1300's significantly reduced the productivity of the individual laborer, and yet wages went *up*. That's because the decreased population also caused a massive drop in competition for land, in turn causing rents to plummet. For more detail on this, read about the Peasants' revolt, also known as Wat Tyler's rebellion (Dyer, 2002).

George says the opposite happened during the reign of Henry VIII, who seized the lands of the church and those held in common by the peasants, and handed them out to newly minted aristocrats, which was followed by suppressed wages.

> *In the reign of Henry VII, half a bushel of wheat would purchase but little more than a day's common labor, but in the latter part of the reign of Elizabeth, half a bushel of wheat would purchase three day's common labor.*

He sums it all up like this:

> *Material progress cannot rid us of our dependence upon land; it can but add to the power of producing wealth from land; and hence, when land is monopolized, it might go on to infinity without increasing wages or improving the conditions of those who have but their labor.*

There's our answer: the monkey wrench that causes the boom-bust cycle of industrial depressions is rent, and even though we have more than enough material wealth to provide for everybody's needs, rent prevents us from distributing it fairly and equitably.

Okay, The Rent Is Too Damn High, and now we finally know why. What are we going to do about it?

9

Insufficiencies of Remedies Currently Advocated

George goes down the list of everything we've already tried and why it hasn't worked, or has worked less well than we hoped:

1. Austerity measures & smaller government

2. Improved education & worker training

3. Labor unions

4. Co-ops

5. Government redistribution of wealth

6. Land redistribution

AUSTERITY & SMALLER GOVERNMENT may help balance the budget, but it is not government spending but rather rent that limits workers' wages.

EDUCATION can help an individual, but when land is monopolized workers still compete with each other for labor. This means if you send everyone to college, all that's changed is now the minimum requirement for every job is a bachelor's degree, and rent still limits wages. What about vocational schools and direct worker training? Even if these are more relevant to teaching skills that raise productivity, the same thing happens: land is monopolized, laborers compete with one another, and rent soaks up the gains.

LABOR UNIONS can increase wages, because they are one of the few forces strong enough to stand against the power of rent. The problem is that unions face a never-ending uphill battle. We often think of "labor versus capital" but what we often call "capital" is just landowners in disguise (because conventional theories include land as a kind of capital). And landowners have a huge structural advantage in negotiations. Labor is the most vulnerable and will quickly starve if idle, but idle capital likewise earns nothing and is actively eaten away by maintenance costs and depreciation. Landowners however can just sit back and collect rent. Given that land is fixed, it is way easier for landowners to collude than it is for either labor or capital (sans land) to unionize.

CO-OPS come in two forms: supplier co-ops and producer/worker-owner co-ops. The former can only lower the cost of exchanges by cutting out middlemen, and the latter just changes the structure of wages (profit-sharing instead of fixed pay). These are good things that help, but don't attack land monopoly and thus can't resist the power of rent.

GOVERNMENT REDISTRIBUTION OF WEALTH through high taxes (presumably income or wealth) have two well-known problems. First, you massively increase the size and scope of government, inviting corruption, an invasive surveillance state, and power-hungry politicians. Second, by taxing income or wealth you're also taxing production, creating "Deadweight loss." Also, given labor and capital can move, if you try to tax them more than they like, they will just

go somewhere else (note that land alone *cannot* do this).
George grants that this kind of brute-force redistributive
policy may well be better than the status quo, but believes
that we can do a lot better. George further predicts that
trying to implement Socialism will lead to demagoguery and
dictatorship in actual practice. He admires the ideal, but says
that such a society must "grow" rather than be
"manufactured."

LAND DISTRIBUTION can and does work to a degree, but
George thinks it still misses the mark a bit. No matter how
you tinker with the rules of who can own land and how or
whether it can be sold, in the long run every system tends
towards the consolidation of land ownership. Even if you go
to the extreme, chop it all up and parcel it out, ownership will
inevitably concentrate again and you'll be back with the same
problem you started with.

Ultimately George says all of these remedies are insufficient
because they don't address the root causes of land monopoly
and do little or nothing to attack the power of rent.

10

The Remedy

George says the solution is to make land common property.

He doesn't want to confiscate land, or force everyone to live on some giant hippie commune. He proposes instead to let everyone continue to "own" land exactly as they do now, but we should impose a special tax to neutralize the perverse incentives of land rent.

He anticipates resistance and promises that the remedy:

1.   Is moral and just

2.   Can actually be practically applied

3.   Will solve all our problems once and for all

WHY THE REMEDY IS MORAL AND JUST

George asks, "what constitutes the rightful basis of property?" What gives you the right to say "this is mine?"

George asserts as self-evident the principle that a person is entitled to the fruits of their labor. What you make on your own time with your own resources, is yours to do with as you please—use it, give it away, trade it, destroy it. You don't harm anyone else doing so.

It follows that neither I nor anyone else am entitled to the product of *your* labor. If we're both independent hunter-gatherers, and you pick some berries from a bush, I don't have any fundamental right to demand them from you.

If you improve land in some way, you're entitled to own and use that, of course. That's the product of your labor. But to claim exclusive and permanent ownership of the land itself— from which all wealth springs and without which labor is impossible—is to demand the product of other's labor. To invoke the sanctity of private property to defend private land ownership is self-refuting.

But what about the right of "I was here first?" Well, George points out that in most cases someone was there before you were, too (and often they were removed by force). Just because you arrived one second, one minute, one year, or one decade before someone else doesn't give you some fundamental right to exclude others from access to nature's free gifts. (Note: this doesn't give people the right to just come in your house and rifle through your underwear drawer at any time of day; we'll get to that).

Now, what about native populations? Isn't this just an excuse for colonialists to come in and steal their land by denying their claim of being on the land first? By George, no—this is a good time to point out that many Native Americans already had a roughly Georgist understanding of land—treating it as common property (Crowfoot, 2021), and it was precisely the colonialists' conception of land as private property that was the motivation for and mechanism by which the indigenous population was expelled and their lands seized.

The English first practiced this on their own people—once upon a time wide swaths of land in England were held in common until the government privatized those lands and gave them out to well-connected gentry in a process called Enclosure (Encyclopaedia Britannica, 2013). If you've ever heard of the Luddites, you should know they weren't merely rebelling against the march of technology, they were also fighting against the forcible seizure of their lands by industrialists (Sale, 1995), who far from being salt-of-the-earth free-enterprise entrepreneurs, were, in actual fact, crony capitalists stealing the people's land with the aid of anti-free-market subsidies and armed thugs, all supported by Big Government™.

As a practical matter though, if you want to impose a Georgist policy, that only applies to territory your state has authority over. Indian reservations in the United States are supposed to be sovereign enclaves with their own jurisdiction. Native Americans can decide for themselves whether they want to adopt any particular policy.

The other reason that the remedy is just is that private ownership of land leads to serfdom.

> *The essence of slavery is that it takes from the laborer all he produces save enough to support an animal existence, and to this minimum the wages of free labor, under existing conditions, unmistakably tend.*

George points out that even though slavery was abolished, the Southern landowners just changed the brand name to "sharecropping" and were able to continue to extract tremendous wealth from "free" Black Americans in the form of rent.

Okay, but excluding evil Southern plantation owners, don't landlords deserve compensation for their work? What about Ms. Nguyen, the nice lady who manages your apartment block and went the extra mile for you when your A/C went out last summer?

I like Ms. Nguyen too, but let's contrast her with Mr. Slumlord, who owns the apartment block next door that's superficially identical, but who *won't* help you when your A/C goes out in the middle of summer.

Ms. Nguyen charges higher "rent" for her much better maintained units because part of that "rent" is actually her justly compensated *wages* for her *labor* in managing them, as well as *interest* from returns on the *capital* she's invested in their ongoing improvement and maintenance. She also collects a good bit of true Georgian rent because she is, after all, a landlord.

Mr. Slumlord puts in as little work as he can get away with and invests as little capital into maintenance as will keep the state off his back. His return is almost entirely *rent*. And the only reason he can charge rent in the first place is because of the valuable location—value the *community* produced, not him.

And that's the real injustice of land rent—the community produces the value, but the landlord charges rent to access it.

PRACTICAL APPLICATION OF THE REMEDY

Okay, land as common property, rent must die, I'm sold. How do we actually do it?

George proposes a Land Value Tax, or LVT.

Note I didn't say *property* tax. Property tax is a tax on the value of a piece of land *and* its improvements. If you're a homeowner, when you pay property tax, you pay tax for *both* the value of your house *and* the lot it is sitting on.

With land value tax you *only* pay tax on the "ground rent," which is the value of your land, but not the improvements.

What's an *improvement?*

By George, a little green house is an improvement. A fancy red hotel is an improvement. A garage, a sidewalk, a public park, a Starbucks, and a hotdog stand are all improvements. Installing a bunch of dikes in the Netherlands and dumping landfill into the seabed to turn wet land into dry is an improvement. All improvements come from labor, and optionally capital, and so it is fair for those factors to take their return. If I "rent" you my hotdog stand (but *not* the lot it sits on) my return would be classified as interest in George's framework because the hotdog stand isn't land, it is capital—the stored-up fruits of my labor that I'm using to get more wealth.

Modified from source, CC BY 2.0 (Taylor, 2012)

The problem with our current system is that when anyone in the community builds improvements, it makes adjoining land more valuable, and then those adjoining landlords jack up the rent. This makes things worse for everybody but the landlords. George's insight is that extra value from my improvement "spills over" from my land and is soaked up by the ground rent of your land.

Under a Land Value Tax, we can correct for the perverse economic incentives, distortions, and oppressions that come from land rent, without having to actually take your land from you.

> *We may safely leave them the shell, if we take the kernel. It is not necessary to confiscate land — only to confiscate rent.*

You also are 100% the owner of the improvements on your land, which *won't* be taxed. This is why Georgism doesn't mean people have the right to barge into your house in the middle of the night even though land is "held in common." Your house is still private property, but the *value* of the land it sits on is common property.

What if I plant some nice trees, and invest in some landscaping to stop erosion? Where's the line between "improvements" and "ground rent?" In most cases it is straightforward to separately assess the value of a plot from the value of what sits on it—modern property tax assessors do this already (Seabury, 2020). George grants that in some edge cases with the passage of time at least some improvements will be subsumed into the land value and that's okay:

> *But it will be said: There are improvements which in time become indistinguishable from the land itself! Very well; then the title to the improvements become blended with the title to the land; the individual right is lost in the common right. It is the greater that swallows up the less, not the less that swallows up the greater.*

Having established that ground rent is bad, how much should we tax it?

By George, *One Hundred Percent.*

Take the rent the tenant has to pay each month, calculate the portion attributable to the value of the unimproved land itself, and send it to the taxing agency.

EFFECTS OF THE REMEDY

Wow! 100% tax rate on ground rent! Can we really do that? In practice Georgists often talk about rates closer to 85% given real-world limitations in assessment, but the point is to hit it as hard as you possibly can. Get close enough and you still have good effects.

Won't land taxes jack up land prices? No, actually—in fact it will do the opposite, because such a tax is laser-calibrated to eliminate speculation, which makes up the bulk of inflated land values, and thus rent. Tax land for the full ground rent and you make real estate *more* affordable, not less. Part III covers the mechanics for how this works in detail, but the short answer for now is that Land Value Tax not only directly decreases the selling price of land, it also causes speculators to flee the market, reducing inflationary demand.

Won't it enable an all-powerful centralized nanny state? Quite the opposite—land value assessment is a fundamentally bottom-up, localized task, so it naturally empowers local municipalities at the expense of distant central authorities. Also, income taxes, wealth taxes, investment taxes, etc., require an ever-vigilant centralized bureaucracy peeking into every aspect of every individual's life to catch tax evaders, who have every incentive to hide their assets or even just flee. Perversely, the IRS currently audits the poor at the same rate as the top 1%, even though higher earners are responsible for withholding the vast majority of tax money in fraud (Kiel, 2019). Land, on the other hand, can't move or hide, and nowadays we have tools like Geographic Information Systems (GIS) to make it even easier to assess. Under Land Value Tax, nobody needs to pry into your personal life or impose burdensome accounting rules on your small business that actually entrench the power of giant corporations, who have entire departments devoted to serving up the Double Irish with a Dutch Sandwich[8].

A Brief Interlude From the Future

Today land value tax is widely considered to be the only tax that doesn't suffer from Deadweight Loss. Deadweight Loss is the lost economic activity or value caused by some policy. It's often summarized by the phrase "If you want less of something, tax it."

Look at the following chart, for example.

---

[8] A tax avoidance scheme that takes advantage of Irish and Dutch tax laws, setting up subsidiaries in those countries and booking profits in low or zero tax jurisdictions to reduce their overall tax obligations (Murphy, 2020).

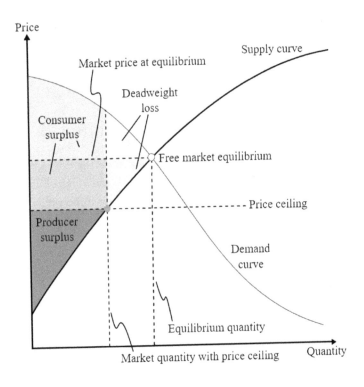

CC BY-SA 2.5 (SilverStar, 2006)

The place where the demand curve (black) and supply curve (gray) meet is the equilibrium point that the market naturally tends towards. But if we impose an artificial price ceiling lower than what the market will bear, the lighter gray area marked "deadweight loss" shows economic activity that can't happen. If you put price controls on gasoline, for instance, you'll get shortages because there's more demand than supply, and supply can't profitably rise to meet the extra bit of demand that's willing to pay a little more.

But here's how things look with a Land Value Tax, notice that the supply curve is now *vertical*—that's weird, what does that mean?

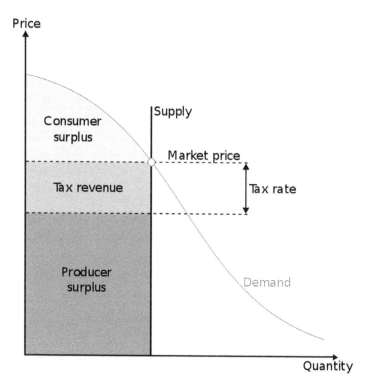

A vertical supply curve means no matter what the price of land is, the same amount will always be supplied. This is because you can't make land—the supply is effectively fixed. Remember, the Netherlands doesn't count because the seabed is land, and filling it in is just an improvement to land that already existed. And even if we granted "The

Netherlands occasionally makes land" for the sake of argument, the amount of land "created" in this way is pretty darn negligible in the grand scheme of the economy, and almost exclusively the domain of governments or state-owned actors.

The supply of land being fixed has some interesting properties. By contrast, consider oil, the supply of which is not fixed. If we tax oil, some of the more marginal wells will be too expensive to operate and make a profit, so producers shut those down and the supply of oil decreases. Deadweight loss comes from a producer's ability to change the amount of product they supply in response to price signals. You'll notice the above graph of land tax has no deadweight loss at all!

Since nobody produces land, it is the one thing you can tax without getting less of it. This drives out speculators entirely. Speculators can no longer distort rents by bidding up the price of land and holding it out of use, and can no longer compete with those who actually intend to *use* the land. A speculator must pay the same taxes as someone who has a productive use for the land. This restores the proper balance of land, labor, and capital.

Now if you work harder, or invest more capital, you can expect to see an increasing return without it all being gobbled up by ever-increasing rent.

If you think about it this way, Land Value Tax has *negative* deadweight loss, because it eliminates the speculative distortion that is the unearned privilege of landownership.

Okay, but won't the landlords just pass the land tax on to their tenants?

By George, no. Rent is a price, and price is governed by supply and demand. Supply of land is fixed, so Land Value Tax has no effect on supply. What about demand? Except in cases where it causes the economy to boom (a good thing), Land Value Tax won't increase land value—what it always does, however, is *reduce* the demand for land by speculators. If it costs nothing to hold on to land, of course I'm going to want to grab some and hold. If the rent I could hope to gain is taxed away, I won't bother.

Consider the case of oil again, where a tax reduces the supply. Reduced supply, given unchanged demand, causes a rise in price. And you'll find the increase in price tracks very closely with the amount of tax.

Land Value Tax is just about the *only* kind of tax that *can't* be passed off to someone else. For more on deadweight loss and the Land Value Tax, see *Welfare Economics of the Land Value Tax* (BlueRepublik, 2019).

Does this mean there can never be profitable landlords ever again? Of course not—they just have to earn their living honestly like everyone else. Remember, we don't tax the *improvements*, just the "ground rent." Ms. Nguyen still gets paid for all her honest work and judicious investments, but Mr. Slumlord doesn't make a dime until he gets off his lazy butt and does something productive.

This is really important, because aside from speculation, the principal cause of land value increase is *the productivity of your neighbors.* An empty lot in the middle of nowhere is worthless, but an otherwise identical empty lot in the middle of New York city is priceless. As they say in real estate—

"location, location, location." The reason location is valuable is because of the activity and contributions of the community, and yet the landlord claims the right to seize all of the economic benefits accruing from the contributions of the community as rent.

Modern economists have some interesting things to say about George's ideas, too. Joseph Stiglitz demonstrated that land rents have a tendency to almost *perfectly equal* the value of investment in public goods. He called this the Henry George Theorem (Stiglitz & Arnott, 1979). Milton Friedman famously called Land Value Tax the "least bad" tax. One of my all-time favorite endorsements will always be the occasion on which the economist Ramin Shokrizade unwittingly re-derived land value tax from first principles to successfully fix recessions in the massively multiplayer online video game EVE Online (Shokrizade, 2013).

Okay, so we tax all the ground rent. It will remove the speculative component of the rent (because there will no longer be any incentive to jack the prices up artificially), but it won't drive the price down to zero. That's because 100% LVT is only achievable on a frictionless plane populated by spherical cows; here in the real world you'll be left with a small sliver of land value. Regardless of the LVT rate, houses and buildings will still have a price. That's fine.

Land in Times Square will still be a lot more *valuable* than land in Podunk, Saskatchewan, but both will approach the same *price* as the LVT rate gets closer to 100%. This encourages people to actually make use of valuable land rather than holding it out of use, blighting the urban core and forcing development to sprawl out for miles in every direction, leading to worse transportation and more pollution.

However, does this mean that if people aren't putting land to productive use, they'll eventually be pressured to sell it off to someone who will?

Yes.

George sees this as a *good* thing. Without Land Value Tax you get situations where somebody can anticipate that an empty lot will become valuable in the future, buy it, hold forever, lobby against future development that would depress their property values, and now you have the Bay Area's housing crisis. Or buy an apartment block, do the absolute minimum the tenants will tolerate without killing you, constantly jack up the rent as the city grows, and you get slums.

As observed in the article "No, Georgism is Still Sane" (BlueRepublik, 2020):

> If you look at the commercial blight in New York City [http://www.vacantnewyork.com/] 90%+ is from landlords refusing to lease out to small businesses, waiting for a larger bank or big business to pay a higher rent bill. This causes property values of nearby businesses to drop, equity value to drop, and businesses to move out from the city center, increasing urban sprawl and urban blight. It's a massive drain on personal wealth, and is very highly linked with poverty and higher crime rates. It's also not a great model for having a stable social fabric.

In a fit of performance art, a Georgist by the name of Fay Lewis once famously bought an empty lot and stuck a big sign on it to demonstrate the principle in action:

"EVERYBODY WORKS BUT THE VACANT LOT"

I paid $3600, for this lot and will hold 'till I get $6000. The profit is unearned increment made possible by the presence of this community and enterprise of its people. I take the profit without earning it. For the remedy read "HENRY GEORGE"

Yours Truly
Fay Lewis

Okay, but isn't building too much stuff bad for the environment? Won't this encourage over-development?

By George, no. What's bad for the environment is *sprawl*, which the current system encourages and which the land tax would directly attack. If you want dense, walkable cities that don't depend on cars to get around, you should eliminate land speculation.

A stronger objection to land value tax is when it is not some shifty speculator or a genocidal English landlord who suffers the brunt of it, but, say, Carl Fredricksen from the beloved Pixar movie *Up.*

The premise of the film is that Carl, a lovably grumpy pensioner, is the last holdout standing in the way of developers bulldozing the rest of his neighborhood in the name of Progress™. He refuses to sell because he can't bear to part with the house which for him is tied up with all the cherished memories of his departed wife. This isn't just sentimental fiction, this is something that really does happen (Vivier, 2017). Isn't Georgism just going to price the poor Carl Fredricksens out of their homes so that someone with a more "productive" use can have it instead?

There are several good responses to this.

For starters, if you're worried about kindly old people losing their homes, that's a thing that's happening already, and most of the time it is because *The Rent Is Too Damn High*, and our existing system is net worse on this score. We are currently facing an unprecedented crisis of evictions (Richter, 2020) in tandem with the COVID pandemic, and it is not like things were peachy before. Even though homelessness seems to be declining in the USA overall, it is getting worse in the most prosperous cities, exactly as George predicted (The Economist, 2019).

Okay, maybe it is better for renters, but what about people who *own* their homes, like Carl? Isn't it unfair to stick them with land taxes that might kick them out? What if they're retired? Remember, let's not confuse land tax with land confiscation, Here's George:

> *I do not propose either to purchase or to confiscate private property in land. The first would be unjust; the second, needless. Let the individuals who now hold it still retain, if they want to, possession of what they are pleased to call their land. Let them continue to call it their land. let them buy and sell, and bequeath and devise it.*

We may safely leave them the shell, if we take the kernel. It is not necessary to confiscate land; it is only necessary to confiscate rent.

Okay, but you have to admit that even if the state isn't confiscating everybody's land, if you can't pay your land taxes you have no choice but to sell your land, right? Isn't this *morally* unjust to the Carl Fredricksens of the world?

First, it is not a given that Mr. Fredricksen will be worse off on net: he already pays income and sales taxes, capital gains on any investments, as well as property tax which taxes both land value *and* the value of his house. As speculators leave the real estate market, the land tax that replaces his property tax will drop, and his house is an improvement, so it would go entirely untaxed.

Also, if the speculators holding onto all the most valuable real estate in the downtown districts are forced to give it up, there won't be as much competition for land and so there's a good chance developers won't be interested in trying to buy up land in a bedroom community in the first place.

BlueRepublik further points out that LVT can be used to fund a Universal Basic Income, which should soften the blow considerably:

Keep in mind also that the Georgist Land Value Tax is paired with a "Citizen's Dividend" or what we see as UBI, so that it's not the government claiming land rent, rather the land rent is taxed and split up equally for all men.

As a matter of political practicality, in the rare event that after all that, Mr. Fredricksen still somehow finds himself in the hole after LVT is applied, Nate Blair suggests a deferment option to grandfather the Carls of the world through the transition:

> *The LVT gets assessed annually for everyone, but owner occupiers (businesses and homeowners) can apply to defer the sum of those payments until they sell or transfer the land. Government can charge a nominal interest.*

If the payments are deferred until death, it's crucial to not allow heirs to "inherit" the deferment. Otherwise a transitional compromise measure turns into a mechanism for anointing a class of permanent landed gentry, similar to the legacy of Proposition 13 in California[9].

A final point of modern application of land value taxes is to level the playing field between different areas by eliminating "cost of living" discrepancies that arise entirely from speculative rent. This is pretty relevant given the "location pay" debate going on in Silicon Valley right now in response to increased remote work as a direct consequence of the COVID pandemic (Hacker News, 2021).

---

[9] A 1978 amendment to the state constitution of California that decreased property taxes by fixing their assessed values to 1976 levels and restricting annual increases in assessments to no more than 2% a year, and the freeze can be passed on to heirs. This is widely considered to be a massive subsidy to existing homeowners and a major driving cause of the ongoing Californian housing crisis. (Friedersdorf, 2018).

Back to George.

Great, we've taxed ground rent at 100% and eliminated speculation and all other manner of social ills. Now what do we *do* with the money?

Lots of things!

For one, you can get rid of some other taxes. Back in George's day it was even argued that a 100% land value tax on ground rents should be the *only* tax—the "Single Tax," replacing all other tariffs, duties, and other taxes (keep in mind this was in the late 1800's and Federal income tax wasn't introduced until the 16th amendment in 1913).

Remember, all these other taxes have deadweight loss. Income tax is a tax on labor, and so taxing it means we really do get less productive labor. The portion of property tax that targets improvements punishes you for investing in improvements, and sales tax is just straight up regressive, hitting the poor harder than the rich.

There's some argument today about whether the "Single Tax" would be enough to fund the modern USA budget, with some Georgists saying it would be sufficient and others saying we would still need some other taxes but could at least significantly offset what we already have.

But by George, another thing we could do is just give all the money back to the people, as BlueRepublik mentioned above. This could be used as a straightforward Universal Basic Income—what was called a "Citizen's Dividend" in George's time, or what Andrew Yang calls the "Freedom Dividend" today. It could also be used for the funding of public goods.

George doesn't see this as an act of charity on the state's behalf—the value of the land has its origin in the productive labors of the entire community, so it is a simple act of distributive justice to give the returns to those who actually produced the value: society at large.

Another effect George asserts is that once land is no longer monopolized, labor is no longer forced into one-sided competition, so wages start to go up. Even better, laborers now have far more opportunity to go into business for themselves, which spurs innovation and investment.

To sum up, if we tax the Dickens out of ground rent, George says we'll see the following benefits:

- It will make housing much more affordable

- It will eliminate perverse incentives and speculation

- It will encourage the most efficient use of land

- It will end wage slavery and rack-rents

- It will encourage investment and innovation

- It will fund a Universal Basic Income and public goods

- It will lower or eliminate some other unpopular taxes

- Finally, it will *not* hand everything over to a centralized planned economy that probably won't work

The Rent is Too Damn High.
But, by George, it doesn't have to be.

PART II

Is Land a Really Big Deal?

11

Why Does Land Matter?

Paul Krugman speaks for many mainstream economists when he admits that Georgist analysis is sound, but he insists that it is a moot point because land just isn't important anymore in the modern economy (Moore, 2017):

> Believe it or not, urban economics models actually do suggest that Georgist taxation would be the right approach at least to finance city growth. But I would just say: I don't think you can raise nearly enough money to run a modern welfare state by taxing land. It's just not a big enough thing.

By George, if land just isn't a big deal, then Land Value Tax can't raise much money, the problems of speculative landownership are vastly overstated, and you can stop reading this book.

The main tension between Georgists on the one hand, and Marxists and Neoclassicals on the other, is that the latter two significantly downplay land, centering the whole discussion instead on labor and capital. For Georgists, land is the key to understanding the whole economy.

Krugman's main complaint is that LVT can't raise enough money, which is a response to the "Single Tax" movement in particular. In George's time, it was popular to advocate for a 100% Land Value Tax *and* the elimination of all other taxes.

Keep in mind that in George's time, there was no federal income tax, and state and federal spending was much lower, so whether LVT could raise enough money wasn't nearly as controversial as it is today.

Even if it turns out that a modern-day "Single Tax" isn't enough to cover the federal budget, Krugman misses the point. The purpose of LVT is not just to raise revenue, but to end speculation, rent-seeking, unaffordable housing, and wasteful, environmentally damaging sprawl. LVT is worth doing for those good effects alone. The revenue it generates doesn't need to fund literally every penny of government spending to still be a win, which is why Georgist economist Terrence Dwyer calls LVT "better than neutral."

Liberal Krugman and conservative Milton Friedman both seem to agree that LVT has no deadweight loss, which means LVT, unlike income and capital taxes, doesn't create a drag on productivity (Friedman, 1978). This means that if we can raise *enough* money from LVT, we can reduce at least some inefficient taxes, such as those on labor, while keeping government spending the same. Not only might this be quite popular politically, but it would also boost the economy.

Those are the claims Georgists make, at least. Let's see if they're true. Here are a few testable hypotheses that capture different aspects of land being a "really big deal:"

1. Most of the value of urban real estate is land

2. USA land rents equal a large share of public spending

3. Land represents a large share of all major bank loans

4.   Land represents a large share of all gross personal assets

5.   Land ownership is concentrated among the wealthy

Note that I'm not trying to prove each of these absolutely unequivocally. I'm just trying to see whether the preponderance of evidence counters the dismissal of land as being only a minor concern in a modern economy.

12

What is Land Value?

For the next few chapters I'm going to empirically establish that land is a big deal, mostly by measuring and estimating land values. But what do I mean by "land value?"

If I have one complaint about *Progress and Poverty*, it is that it ironically doesn't spend *enough* time beating words to absolute death. "Land Value" in particular is one of the terms that could use some clarifying, because it has conflicting definitions depending on how it is being used.

For example: when some people hear "100% Land Value Tax," they imagine it means that if they paid $10,000 for a piece of land, they will owe $10,000 a year in "Land Value Taxes," which feels absurd. Indeed it is—what "100% Land Value Tax" *really* means, is that if that same piece of land can be rented for $500 a month apart from anything built on it, the owner owes $500 a month in Land Value Taxes. "Land value" in this context means the *rental* value of the land, not the selling price.

LAND (RENTAL) VALUE is the *recurring income* land is capable of generating from the market, whether or not said income is actually being collected as money or not. This income[10] (also known as "land rent," "ground rent," or "geo-rent") is the recurring price people are willing to pay for the exclusive use of the land alone, apart from any improvements like buildings. People are willing to pay to use the land because of its desirable location as well as any natural attributes, such as agricultural fertility, topography, endowment of water, minerals, etc.

Rental value is related to, but distinct from, *selling* value.

LAND (SELLING) VALUE is just the price of the land in a sale. "Full selling value," however, has a special meaning, a term equivalent to "full market value" in modern real estate assessment. When we speak of "full" market or selling value, we specifically mean the price a property would fetch in a free and open market at an arms-length sale, between well informed, uncoerced parties. In other words, the "full selling value" of the land is its purchase-price under "fair" and open market conditions, whereas generic "selling value" is whatever it just sold for, regardless of the conditions.

Here's an example: let's say your dad has a valuable property. He could sell it on the open market and get up to $10,000 for it, but he decides instead to "sell" it to you, his child, for $1, essentially as a gift. The naïve selling value is $1, but the "full selling value" would be the highest price the open market would happily pay for this land—$10,000.

---

[10] This also includes "imputed" rents—the money an owner-occupier avoids paying to a landlord as rent because they are their own landlord, and thus effectively pay rent to themselves.

Land Value Tax intends to capture rental value, not the selling value. It's not a tax on the market purchase price of a property, nor is it a fixed amount of tax per acre of land regardless of location or quality, but rather a tax which redirects the flow of land rents.

LVT should not be confused with a property tax. Property taxes considers land plus improvements (typically buildings). An LVT considers land rental value alone.

Now that we've established all that, let's move on to demonstrating that land is a big deal.

13

Most Urban Real Estate Value is Land

It's more expensive to live in the heart of New York City than in the middle of Nebraska. That's not because construction costs are orders of magnitude more expensive in New York, but because the land is orders of magnitude more expensive.

Here's a map of land prices across America's 100 largest metro areas, courtesy of the American Enterprise Institute. Notice that the most valuable properties are situated in coastal urban areas (American Enterprise Institute, 2021):

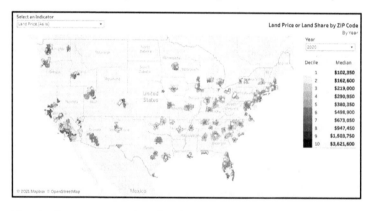

Here's the same map but for *land share*—the percentage of a property's value that's due solely to the land. If you build a shack in the desert, nearly 100% of the property's value will come from the shack, because the land is worthless. But if you build a shack in San Francisco, nearly all of the property's value will come from the land. Notice how the land share gets closer to 100% as you move towards big cities along the coast.

This is because of increased demand for land near large population centers and areas with significant economic activity and commerce. The increased value of the land is not due to any individual, but to the collective inputs of the entire community in developing the area around it. This is often called the "agglomeration effect."

Even so, maybe you don't trust the American Enterprise Institute's figures and want to hear from some other people.

In 2014, the "developable land" on Manhattan island alone was estimated to be worth about $1.74 trillion (just the land) (Barr, Smith, & Kulkarni, 2018).

Between 2005-2010, the urban land (selling) value for *all* of New York City was about $2.5 trillion (just the land) (Albouy, Ehrlich, & Shin, Metropolitan Land Values, 2017).

In 2020, all real estate in NYC was estimated to be worth about $2.7 trillion (the land + the buildings) (Kapfidze, 2020).

But let's go ahead and see for ourselves. You can run a quick spot check by going on real estate sites like Zillow or Redfin in a major city like New York or San Francisco. First, search for a vacant lot for sale in the heart of downtown, and note the asking price. Then look for a similarly-sized lot with a building on it that has sold within the last few years, situated next to the empty lot. The last selling price should be available. You can subtract one price from the other to get a rough estimate of the land share of the plot with the building on it.

Here's a Redfin listing for a vacant lot in the heart of San Francisco (personal information redacted). They're asking for $1.99 million dollars, and, judging from other listings and sales records in the area, they'll probably get it.

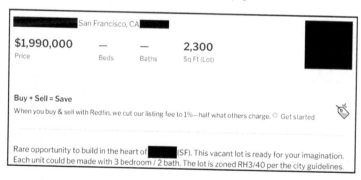

San Francisco, CA			
$1,990,000	—	—	**2,300**
Price	Beds	Baths	Sq Ft (Lot)

Buy + Sell = Save
When you buy & sell with Redfin, we cut our listing fee to 1%—half what others charge. ○ Get started

Rare opportunity to build in the heart of ▮▮▮ (SF). This vacant lot is ready for your imagination. Each unit could be made with 3 bedroom / 2 bath. The lot is zoned RH3/40 per the city guidelines.

Here's a townhouse right next door that sold last year, situated on a lot of nearly the same size. We're ignoring the "Redfin Estimate;" all we care about is the "this home last sold for" figure at the bottom, which is about $2.4 million.

███████ San Francisco, CA ████				███
$2,320,106 Redfin Estimate	**3** Beds	**3.5** Baths	**2,020** Sq Ft	
Off Market This home last sold for $2,395,000 on ████ 2020.				

This is all the information we need for our spot check. First, we adjust for size. The second property's lot is 88% as big as the vacant lot, so we multiply the vacant lot's value ($1.99 million) by 88% to get $1.75 million. Now we subtract: $2.32 million - $1.75 million = $568,000, the presumptive value of the building. That suggests that 24% of the total property value is from the building, and 76% is from the land. This is just napkin math, but it is congruent with the 70.9% figure AEI gives for the average land share of property in San Francisco county in 2020.

Our spot check confirms the findings from the studies and AEI's dataset. Real estate in urban areas is expensive because of land, and the most valuable land is in urban areas.

If you don't believe me, I have an empty lot in Gerlach, Nevada to sell you (Land Equities, 2020). Don't worry—it only costs $0.0054/sqft. Meanwhile, our empty lot in San Francisco is going for $865.21/sqft, which is over 159,000 times as expensive.

Given the evidence from the various land value estimation studies and databases like AEI's, as well as how easy it is to run spot checks, I'm convinced.

CONCLUSION:
Most of the value of urban real estate is, in fact, land.

14

How Much is All of America's Land Worth?

Krugman and other skeptics don't believe you can raise enough with LVT alone to fund a modern state. Noah Smith, on the other hand, claims that "Land is underrated as a source of wealth" (Smith N. , 2018). Regardless of who's right, LVT doesn't need to replace all other taxes to still be worth doing, as long as it can raise a significant enough chunk. How much can it raise? Let's do the math and find out.

SPOILER ALERT:
Conservative estimates show that we can entirely pay for any one of the following: Defense, Social Security, or Medicare + Medicaid, using land rents alone. Optimistic estimates suggest that we're within striking distance of the Single Tax—replacing all labor and capital taxes with taxes on land rents (on the federal level, at least).

MATH ALERT:
We're about to dive into all the research papers and calculations that back up the above statement. If you don't care about seeing me show my work and you want to jump right to the conclusion, go ahead and skip to the next chapter, *How Much Money Can We Raise From Land Rents?*

Let's start by defining certain terms very precisely again:

To recap, *land income* or *land rent* is the recurring amount of revenue that the land itself is capable of generating. It's the market value that derives from the benefits the land itself provides (crops it can grow, proximity to a desirable job, etc.) and the most anybody is willing to pay to access that land for a while (conventional "rent.") It is ultimately land income that drives land selling value, not the other way around.

Land price or *land selling value* is how much it costs to buy a piece of land. *Full market selling value,* however, is specifically the land price under "fair" and open market conditions (what it would fetch in an open sale, not a $1 transfer from your dad, or a coerced bargain sale to someone who's blackmailing you.)

So how much *is* all the land in America worth? Or more precisely, what is the *full market selling value* of all of America's land?

I have put together a graph of America's total aggregate land selling value over time, according to twelve different estimation methods. My sources are The Lincoln Institute of Land Policy (2017), Larson (2015), Albouy, Ehrlich, & Shin (2017), The American Enterprise Institute (2021), PLACES Lab (2020), the Federal Reserve (2000-2020) via a method worked out by Matt Yglesias (2013), Larson, Davis, Oliner, & Shui (2019-2020), and Jeffrey Johnson Smith's book, *Counting Bounty: The Quest to Know the worth of the Earth* (2020).

Put all their estimates together on one chart and you get this:

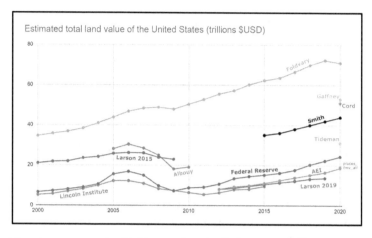

The data points for Foldvary, Smith, Tideman, Gaffney and Cord all come from *Counting Bounty*. Smith gives his own estimate of $44 trillion and notes an estimate of $31 trillion that Nicolaus Tideman sent him via private correspondence (which I confirmed by e-mailing Tideman).

Smith further mentions that Fred Foldvary was constantly saying that land rents equal about 1/3 of national income, and a cursory googling of Foldvary's writings confirms this. The "Foldvary" line here is my own construction that takes a third of Gross National Income (St. Louis Fed, 2021) for each year and then multiplies it by 10 (Smith's method for converting land rents to land selling value). Smith also cites a land rent estimate by Mason Gaffney at $5.3 trillion, or $53 trillion in total value, though I've not been able to track down the primary source for that. Finally, I've extrapolated Smith's estimate five years back from his single 2020 data point according to the observed growth line from the other data sets.

That gives us a massive spread of anywhere between $19 trillion to $65 trillion in 2020 for all of America's land values.

Whom do we trust here?

Let's start from the top with Foldvary's estimate. Foldvary is looking at the results of a 2003 paper by Terrence Dwyer in Australia, and then saying that the same pattern Dwyer notes is likely to hold in America.

For context, Terrence Dwyer is a Georgist who spent several years as an Australian Treasury tax official, was an advisor to the Prime Minister and Cabinet, and has written extensively about tax policy. His paper is called *The Taxable Capacity of Australian Land and Resources* (Dwyer, 2003).

Unlike America, Australia has a long history of land taxation and detailed land valuation records, which Dwyer uses to put together four tables comparing land incomes to all Australian tax receipts. Although Australia has a history of land valuation and LVT that continues to this day, they fall far short of maximum Georgism, relying on quite a bit of conventional capital and labor taxes.

Here are some figures from the most recent decade in Dwyer's fourth table, which shows that land rents could raise 70-75% as much as all of Australia's other taxes combined.

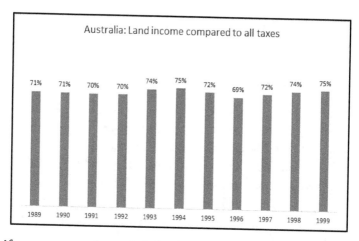

If you compare Australia's land income to the receipts taken in just by Australia's company and personal income taxes, it would be more than enough to replace them entirely while still bringing in a surplus.

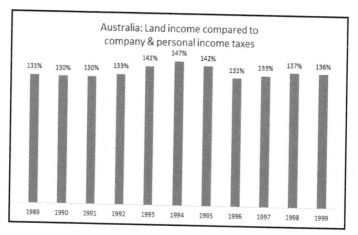

Dwyer's methodology seems plausible; it is a straightforward application of Australia's detailed land and property value records against Australia's published budget figures. Dwyer notably *doesn't* factor in the potential revenue from the "dynamic effects" of Land Value Taxation, which would only serve to raise his figures. Great news for Australia, at least if you believe Dwyer and his data sources.

Let's check the ratio of Australian land rents to Australian national income and see if it matches Foldvary's "one-third" claim. In 1999, Dwyer gives Australia's land income as $132.7 billion AUD (Australian dollars). In 1999, Australian GNI (gross national income) was $405.5 billion USD (*American* dollars), and, using the 1999 conversion rate, that's $623.9 billion AUD (macrotrends, 2022). That gives a land-rent-to-GNI ratio of 21.3%. Spot-checking 1991 gives me 20.8%, so the figure didn't change much over time.

These Australian figures are pretty far off from Foldvary's "one-third" guess, but pretty close to Steven Cord's. Cord estimated land rent at about 24% of national income (Barron, 1988). That would be about $47 trillion using Smith's method. Given Foldvary is contradicted by his own source, Dwyer, we should probably exclude Foldvary's line for now and construct a new one for Cord, as well as a "Dwyer-USA" line using 21% of America's GNI to better represent what Foldvary was originally getting at.

If we buy that the Australian pattern might hold for the United States, our new chart looks something like this:

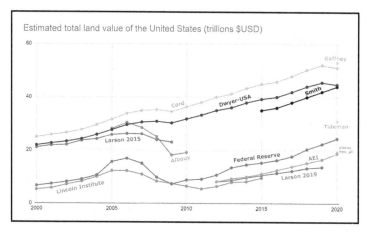

Because the Cord and Dwyer-USA lines are just naively tracking GNI, they somewhat mask the 2005-2008 housing bubble. Nevertheless, they give something like an upper bound. Taking it all in, we see three emerging clusters of lines. Could this reflect a difference in methodologies?

Indeed.

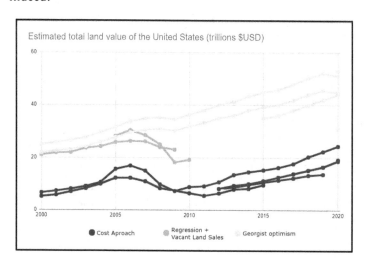

In Part IV, we'll dig into how to accurately assess land values in detail, but for now, let's look at the broad strokes differences between the estimation methods used here.

The bearish values in black all rely on a method called the "cost approach," or "land residual" method. This is where you take the estimated cost it would take to replace a building, multiply that against depreciation based on the building's age, and then subtract that from the total market value of the property to get the land value.

Larson (2019) uses this method, and AEI's figures are based directly on those results with a slight upward correction. The Lincoln Institute and the Federal Reserve's figures use the same basic approach, relying on official estimates of construction costs and housing prices. The one outlier is the PLACES lab estimate, which uses a machine learning model but gives a single-year result that tracks with the four cost approach lines.

The bullish values in light gray all come from estimates by various Georgists cited in Smith's book. I have naively back-extrapolated them just to set an upper bound.

The middle values in medium gray include Larson (2015), who uses a "hedonic regression" model, and Albouy, who builds a model that *only* looks at vacant land sales.

Long story short, I found numerous persuasive criticisms of the cost approach. Ultimately, I think Smith's estimate is most likely closest to the truth. Let's dig into Larson, Albouy, and the Federal Reserve figures to understand why.

A TALE OF TWO LARSONS

Larson disagrees with himself. Let me grey out most of the other lines to highlight this discrepancy:

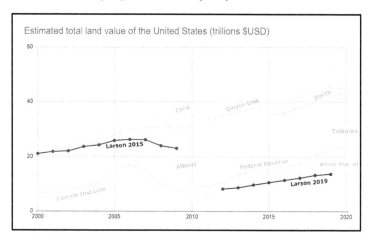

Larson (2015) was written by Larson alone and uses a "hedonic regression" approach similar to the one described in a paper by Kuminoff and Pope (2013). In this method, you note all the characteristics of a property and then use a computer model to tease out the individual contributions of each factor to the final market value. This paper's data comes from a variety of sources but includes vacant land sales, developed property sales, and official stats from appraisals.

Larson (2019), on the other hand, was co-written with Davis, Oliner, and Shui and uses the cost approach exclusively. Crucially, Larson (2019) explicitly and intentionally *excludes* all vacant land sales from the dataset. This estimate thus has the *least* direct contact with ground truth data from the market concerning land.

ALBOUY'S ASTOUNDING APPENDIX

I think we can all agree that the purest way to measure the selling value of land is to find a piece of land with nothing on it and observe the price it sells for on the market. With enough of these data points, you could interpolate between them to create a smooth gradient map of land values, which could be good enough for estimating the aggregate value of large areas.

Unfortunately, this method isn't going to work to model urban (selling) land values because there just aren't enough pure-land sales in the city center. Or are there?

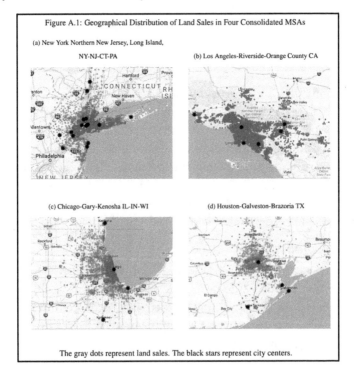

Figure A.1: Geographical Distribution of Land Sales in Four Consolidated MSAs

(a) New York Northern New Jersey, Long Island, NY-NJ-CT-PA

(b) Los Angeles-Riverside-Orange County CA

(c) Chicago-Gary-Kenosha IL-IN-WI

(d) Houston-Galveston-Brazoria TX

The gray dots represent land sales. The black stars represent city centers.

This startling figure is from the online appendix to Albouy's paper, briefly referenced in a footnote in the main paper. Apparently, there are *more* pure land sales in urban areas than there are in outlying areas. As far as I can tell, Albouy builds his statistical model using *nothing* but pure land sales, excluding anything that has a structure on it. Surprisingly, his data points are most densely clustered around major city centers, when I had expected this approach would yield the exact opposite.

Both Albouy and Larson (2015) use regression models that include vacant land sales, but Albouy *only* considers vacant land sales. By contrast, Larson (2019) uses the cost approach and explicitly *excludes* vacant land sales. What about the Federal Reserve Method?

THE FUZZY FED

The "Federal Reserve" line is my own construction. Matthew Yglesias described this method in *What's All the Land in America worth?* in 2013, arriving at $15 trillion. In this method, you look at the balance sheets on the Federal Reserve's annual Flow of Funds report and subtract the replacement values of all structures from the total value of real estate holdings. There's good reason to believe this method produces estimates that are too low.

Smith spends a lot of time attacking the Federal Reserve's figures, with arguments similar to Michael Hudson's critique from a 2001 article called *Where Did All the Land Go?* Here's Hudson:

When the Fed's methodology was examined on a sector by sector basis, serious problems were found in the breakdown between land and structures. For instance, by 1993 the FRB estimated that the land held by all nonfinancial corporations had a negative value of $4 billion.

This does, in fact, check out. The Fed was apparently so embarrassed by this that they stopped reporting land value estimates in subsequent reports, which is why you now have to derive them yourself. This raises two questions: 1) are these problems still in effect today, and 2) if the Fed was so incompetent in the past, how can we trust that later estimates are not just as wrong, but in the other direction, i.e. wildly *over*-stated land selling values?

Based on Smith and Hudson's critiques, as well as my own analysis of the data, the answers seem to be that: 1) the problems seem less bad today (no more negative land values!) but are probably still present to some degree, and 2) any bias is most likely in the downward direction.

The reason for this has to do with the limitations of the cost approach, a problem many of these papers raise explicitly—including Larson (2019). Buildings naturally depreciate over time, while land tends to appreciate. The cost to *replace* your building with a new one of identical design is on average going to be a lot more than what your old building is actually worth, even after factoring in depreciation. That's because the market doesn't care what you spent to build it, it only cares how much value it provides under current conditions. Here's a contrived example. Say you built an amusement park for $10 million ten years ago, and now prospective buyers want to tear it down and build apartments on it. Your roller coasters aren't worth $10 million minus ten years depreciation; they're worth zero, even if they're still in decent shape. That's because now there's a shinier and better amusement park down the road that's driven you nearly out of business, and none of your prospective buyers are interested in operating an amusement park. All they want is the land. Your structures might even have *negative* value because it costs money to tear them down.

In short, the cost approach is flawed because subtracting the inflated building price from the full market value of the property overvalues structures and undervalues land.

But what about the other figure in the equation—the full market value of the real estate (land + buildings)? If the Federal Reserve is basing those figures off of assessed values, we have good reason to believe they are too low. For one, only a minority of US states and Canadian provinces re-assess property values annually (IAAO, 2017):

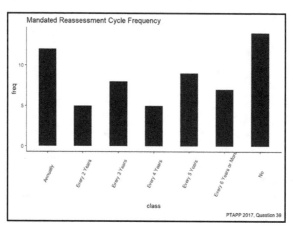

For another, property tax assessments have all kinds of
exemptions and carve-outs that serve to depress official
statistics. Let's put aside the legacy of Proposition 13 in
California for a second and compare Redfin's history of sales
and tax records for properties like this one from Manhattan:

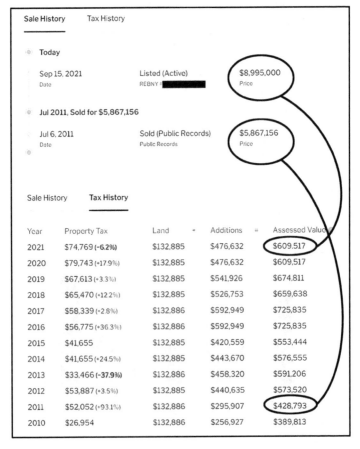

| **Sale History** | **Tax History** | | | | |

Today			
Sep 15, 2021	Listed (Active)		$8,995,000
Date	REBNY # ███████		Price

Jul 2011, Sold for $5,867,156			
Jul 6, 2011	Sold (Public Records)		$5,867,156
Date	Public Records		Price

| Sale History | **Tax History** | | | |

Year	Property Tax	Land	+	Additions	=	Assessed Value
2021	$74,769 (-6.2%)	$132,885		$476,632		$609,517
2020	$79,743 (+17.9%)	$132,885		$476,632		$609,517
2019	$67,613 (+3.3%)	$132,885		$541,926		$674,811
2018	$65,470 (+12.2%)	$132,885		$526,753		$659,638
2017	$58,339 (+2.8%)	$132,886		$592,949		$725,835
2016	$56,775 (+36.3%)	$132,886		$592,949		$725,835
2015	$41,655	$132,885		$420,559		$553,444
2014	$41,655 (+24.5%)	$132,885		$443,670		$576,555
2013	$33,466 (-37.9%)	$132,886		$458,320		$591,206
2012	$53,887 (+3.5%)	$132,885		$440,635		$573,520
2011	$52,052 (+93.1%)	$132,886		$295,907		$428,793
2010	$26,954	$132,886		$256,927		$389,813

Assessed values less than 10% of the extremely obvious full market value.

It sold for 5.8 million 10 years ago, and now it is listed for 9 million. And yet the "assessed value" is a mere $600K. What's going on? The assessor is probably *not* saying that the full market value of this obviously multi-million-dollar property is $600K. Most likely the assessor gave their best guess of "full market value," and then state statutes forced the assessor to also write down a separate "assessed value" that applies some markdown percentage. The really damning part of these tax assessment records is that the land value assessment hasn't budged. The price has gone up over 3 million dollars in ten years, and you're telling me the land selling value hasn't changed at *all? Fuhgeddaboudit!*

Agencies that don't collect much property tax don't have strong incentives to strive for accurate assessments. This creates a vicious cycle where official statistics are severely depressed, and those same statistics are then used as proof that land just isn't a big deal.

If the Federal Reserve's data for total real estate values is at all based on property values from official sources, we would expect them to be 1) out of date and 2) discounting the property's total market value because of exemptions, caps, and other issues (Smith makes this same critique of both the Fed and Larson's data as well.)

Taken together with the fact that improvements are likely being over-valued based on naïve replacement costs + depreciation formulas instead of the actual present market value, this would imply that the Federal Reserve method for estimating all of America's land selling values at $24 trillion is a *conservative lower bound,* and the same goes for all the other methods using the cost approach.

FROM ALBOUY TO SMITH

Okay, so let's look at Jeffrey Johnson Smith's method.
Instead of doing a whole new study, he singles out Albouy as
having the best methodology and makes some adjustments.
You see, Albouy estimated the value of urban land *alone,*
leaving out federal lands, agricultural lands, and things like
water rights and natural resources, which accrue rental
income and are considered "Economic Land" by Georgists.

Smith starts by extrapolating Albouy's last given figure to the
present day by applying the observed growth in the housing
market (presumably due to appreciation of land selling
values). He then adds on values for the missing types of land
by using other existing estimates. It all comes to $44 trillion.

We can check his work pretty quickly. All the figures we have
for the last decade that don't come from Smith grow at a very
similar rate, with the Federal Reserve line growing at a steady
~$1.4 trillion a year on average. Let's extrapolate Albouy at
the same rate:

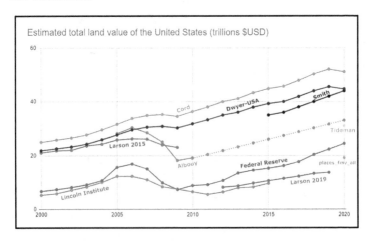

Interestingly enough, that puts us just over Tideman's estimate but short of Smith's final value by about $11 trillion. The average value of farm land was $3,160 per acre in 2020 (USDA, 2020). Multiply that by 896.6 million acres (Shahbandeh, 2021) and you get $2.8 trillion dollars. Smith further cites Richard Ebeling, who in 2015 estimated the value of all of the federal government's holdings in land and mineral reserves at $5.5 trillion dollars (Ebeling, 2015). Smith applies an extrapolation to update this value to 2020, putting it at $6.6 trillion.

If we just pop $2.8 trillion + $6.6 trillion on top of the extrapolated line from Albouy, that gives us this:

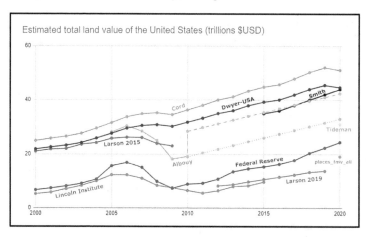

Which gets us pretty close to Smith's figure. The USDA figure seems reliable, because most farmland doesn't have structures on it and is just pure land. The USDA can value the land just by observing market transactions. As for Ebeling, you kind of have to take his word for it, as he doesn't give a methodology. Ebeling is also a hardcore libertarian who advocates selling off all federal lands to reimburse taxpayers (wonder how he'd feel seeing Smith use his estimates to advocate Georgism!). In any case, if you buy all of that, you get pretty close to Smith's $44 trillion figure, which is itself close to Dwyer's observed ratio in Australia of land rents as 21% of national income (provided you use Smith's 10:1 ratio to convert land rents to land selling values).

Of the original studies, Albouy has the most convincing methodology, and Smith's additions and extrapolations seem plausible. To be fair, let's set Smith ($44 trillion) as an upper bound, and the Federal Reserve figure ($24 trillion) as a lower bound.

I should note here that a lot of this land is already paying property taxes, which is at least partially a Land Value Tax. Research shows that Land Value Taxes are "capitalized" into land prices. I'll explain this in Part III, but for now, suffice it to say that if an income-generating piece of land produced $10,000 a year for you, and you knew you had to pay $5,000 a year for the privilege of holding it, you'd probably only be willing to buy it for half as much as you would if the tax didn't exist. Since the point of this exercise is to estimate how much a blanket LVT could raise, a more rigorous study would work out how much present land prices have been depressed by existing land taxes and adjust these figures upwards accordingly to get a more accurate estimate of the full land rents. Long story short, this gives us good reason to believe that the true figures for land selling values are higher than all those presented here, regardless of methodology.

LAND VALUES VS. LAND RENTS

Now we have to convert land selling values to land rents—the amount of income the land is capable of generating each year.

To convert between land selling values and land rents, we need to use the capitalization rate, or "cap rate." If your land costs $1 million and earns $50,000 per year, the cap rate is $50,000 / $1,000,000, or 5%. This is the ratio between the net operating income produced by a plot of land ($50,000) and its market value ($1 million).

According to various sources (Arbor, 2021) (CBRE, 2019) (CBRE, 2020), cap rates in the US range between 3.5% on the low end to as much as 11% on the high end, depending on the type of property (offices have a higher rate, residential has a lower rate, etc.). However, the vast majority of land selling values in the United States are urban, so we should weight our cap rates towards urban figures. Call it a low of 5% and a high of 8%. Smith suggests using a blanket cap rate of 10%, but I'm erring on the conservative side.

The 2005 federal budget had $2.5 trillion in expenditures, increasing to $4.4 trillion in 2019, with a sharp jump to $6.6 trillion in 2020 thanks to COVID (Peters, 2021). It's immediately clear that regardless of valuation method, America's total land selling values ($24-44 trillion) are significantly higher than the annual federal budget. But we care about land *rents*. It's not like the plan is to sell off all of America's land just to pay for a few years' spending.

If we plug in the figures from the Federal Reserve and Smith, that gives us the following figures for America's annual land rents (in trillions of dollars):

SOURCE	YEAR	5%	6.5%	8%
Federal Reserve	2017	0.8	1.2	1.4
Federal Reserve	2018	1.0	1.3	1.6
Federal Reserve	2019	1.1	1.4	1.8
Federal Reserve	2020	1.2	1.6	1.9
Smith	2017	1.9	2.5	3.0
Smith	2018	2.0	2.6	3.2
Smith	2019	2.1	2.7	3.4
Smith	2020	2.2	2.9	3.5

With that, we have constructed a table that tells us, roughly speaking, how much money the LVT might be able to raise. Keep in mind even the optimistic figures don't account for dynamic effects and aren't necessarily pricing in all other sources of "Economic Land" such as mineral rights, water rights, etc. They also don't apply any estimates for how much land selling values would rise if restrictive zoning ordinances were removed, or if we factored out the capitalized value of existing property taxes, all of which would serve to raise these figures.

Now we just need to compare that to America's budget figures.

15

How Much Money Can Land Rents Raise?

America's annual land rents are sufficient to cover between 18%-40% (Fed) and 34-78% (Smith) of annual federal spending. The low-end figures come from 2020, which was a major outlier in federal spending thanks to COVID.

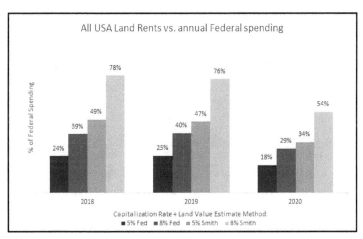

All USA Land Rents vs. annual Federal spending

To put those amounts in context, in the 2019 federal budget, total spending was $4.4 trillion (Congressional Budget Office, 2020). We spent $676 billion on defense (15%), Social Security was $1 trillion (23%), and Medicare + Medicaid together were $1.05 trillion (24%). Let's compare those to our four individual estimates for annual land rental values:

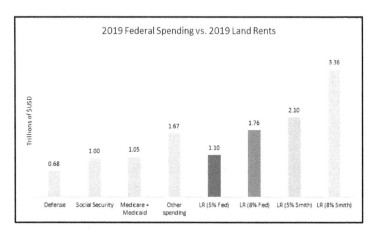

Even the lowest estimate, the Federal Reserve method using a 5% cap rate, is enough to cover any one of Defense, Social Security, or Medicare + Medicaid, all by itself. And if you believe Smith's figure at the 8% cap rate, we could cover *all three of those things* and still have enough left over to cover a third of all other spending.

Here's another point of comparison. There are 745 billionaires in America, and some people think we should tax them to pay for all our stuff (Kulish, Livni, & Emma, 2021). As obscenely rich as billionaires are, the amount of money it takes to run a country at scale is even more obscene. If we were to "eat the rich" and forcibly expropriate 100% of billionaires' money, we would raise a one-time lump sum of about $5 trillion. That's a lot! But land rents by comparison can raise between 22-44% as much *every single year,* and that's at the low cap rate.

This is not necessarily an argument against taxes on billionaires, mind you (I have no problem with the rich paying their fair share.) It's simply meant to show that land rents represent a lot more value than people realize, and, unlike one-time personal wealth expropriations, they recur annually. Furthermore, land, unlike capital, can't flee the country and take investment and industry with it.

Fun fact: taking all the billionaires' money yields a little less than selling off all of America's federal lands and mineral reserves (Ebeling's estimate). Whether or not you opt for the right-libertarian hobby horse (sell federal lands) or the leftist one (eat the rich), either could at best pay for a single year's spending on the scale of 2020's budget.

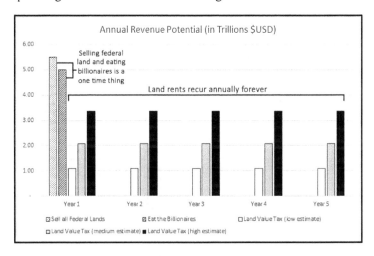

What about state budgets (NASBO, 2021)? Many states are funded by property taxes, so if we're going to shift to land value taxes, we need to take states into account, too. Let's add state budgets into the mix (minus federal funding to states so we're not double counting). If we do that, we drop to 18-30% (Fed) or 36-58% (Smith) of annual spending.

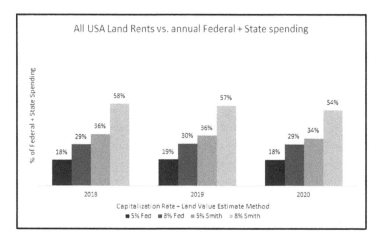

If we look ONLY at net spending from all state budgets (all 50 state government outlays minus federal funding to states), you could cover anywhere from 67-121% (Fed) or 142-230% (Smith) with land rents, implying that states—particularly the ones with big cities—could easily fund themselves off of LVT alone.

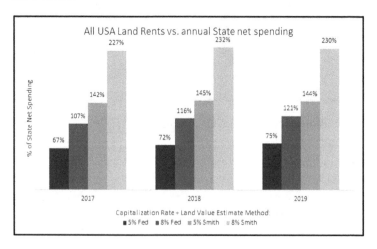

Now let's look at this another way. The federal government hasn't run a balanced budget since that one time in 1998 (Planes, 2013), so the proper way to evaluate LVT against the status quo isn't comparing against total annual expenditures, but against total annual tax *receipts* (revenue).

By this measure, all of America's land rents could cover anywhere from 30-56% (Fed) or 60-103% (Smith) of what our current tax receipts bring in.

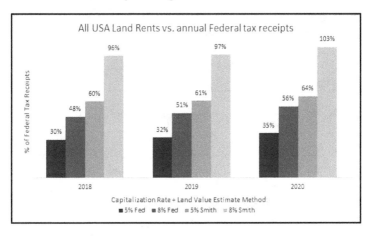

And if you add in state tax receipts too, you get somewhere between 19-36% (Fed) and 41-68% (Smith). I couldn't find a source for state tax receipts, but most states are required to run balanced budgets, so I'm just assuming that the state budget expenditure figures from above are the same as their receipts. If I had more precise figures from the few states that do run deficits, that would only serve to reduce the assumed amount of tax receipts from those states, which could only raise the percentages given here:

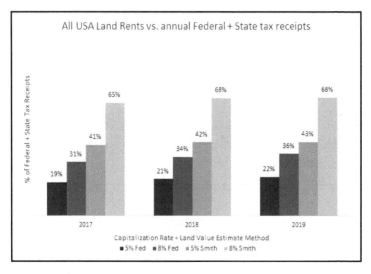

Finally, what about local governments (Airi, Dadayan, & Rueben, 2021)? That's where a lot of the property taxes currently go anyways (not to mention regressive taxes like sales taxes and lotteries.) If we add in all their tax money too, and compare it to annual land rents, that drops us to 14-26% (Fed) or 29-49% (Smith) of annual receipts.

Keep in mind, however, that this doesn't account for property values that already have state and local property tax burdens priced into them. If we were to factor that in, it would raise these figures significantly.

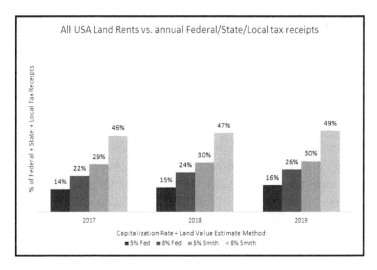

No matter how you slice it, the most low-end estimate of 14-26% of all federal, state, *and* local tax receipts is a lot of money, especially when you consider that it recurs annually and can cover any single giant line-item in the federal budget. On the higher end, Smith's 29-49% figure for land rents compared to *all tax receipts for every level of government combined* would be astounding.

Restricting ourselves to just the federal level, Smith's 60-103% figure is more than enough to entirely eliminate individual income taxes on the low end (about 50% of federal receipts in 2019 (U.S. Government Publishing Office, 2019)) and is in clear striking distance of a full-on Federal Single Tax on the high end.

Of course, if you think Smith is wrong and the Federal Reserve's figures have it nailed, then the Single Tax dream might be out of reach.

How big a deal this is depends on what you think about balanced budgets.

If you believe in Modern Monetary Theory, then you don't care about running a balanced budget. Under MMT, a sovereign government that prints its own money is limited only by productive capacity and physical resources, summed up best by the famous Keynes quote, "anything we can actually *do* we can afford" (Keynes, 1978). I'm not personally advocating for or against this view—just pointing out that if you're in the MMT camp, then you already don't care about matching 100% of government spending with revenue raised from taxes.

But what if MMT is bunk, and if we also insist on the Fed's figures? Then we're left with two options: either accept that doctrinaire Single-Taxism is done for (in the US, at least) while still accepting LVT as part of this balanced budget breakfast, or else look into those "dynamic effects" that Dwyer's Australian figures intentionally left out, particularly a tantalizing theory most commonly associated with Mason Gaffney. Gaffney, a famous and prolific Georgist economist and professor, called this theory ATCOR—"All Taxes Come Out of Rents" (Gaffney 2005).

ATCOR AND THE HENRY GEORGE THEOREM

The ATCOR hypothesis states that any reduction in taxes on income and capital (assuming you hold all other policies constant) will cause a proportionate increase in land selling values. Effectively, the extra money returning to the economy from tax cuts will get soaked up by rising rent.

This means that Georgists who suppose that any old LVT policy will cause land prices to go down need to be careful. If you un-tax labor and capital, but don't *also* sufficiently raise taxes on land, land prices (and rents) will actually go *up,* because someone working on that land is now taking home more income and therefore capable of paying more in rent (see Ricardo's Law of Rent). However, with the right policy, this can be a good thing.

If ATCOR is true, a Single Tax policy will always work. Abolishing capital and income taxes causes the lost tax revenue to get soaked up by rising land rental values, which you can then capture with a 100% LVT. You're raising the exact same amount of revenue as before, but the elimination of income and capital taxes lifts a burden off of labor and investment while LVT keeps housing prices and rents down, avoiding speculative bubbles while boosting the economy and lowering the cost of living. This economic boost in turn raises land rental values, which are fully captured by LVT, thus keeping land selling values low.

Then there's the Henry George Theorem. Nobel laureate Joseph Stiglitz published it in 1979, and it says that under certain conditions, expenditures on public goods will be soaked up by land rents to such a degree that a 100% LVT is *necessarily* sufficient to finance all public goods spending in perpetuity (Stiglitz & Arnott, 1979).

Consider first that under the status quo, the bulk of spillover value created by public spending is captured by private landowners. Governments then have to tax citizens' labor and capital to pay for the next round of improvements or else go into debt with deficit spending and bond initiatives (a hidden tax on savings if it causes inflation). The Henry George theorem suggests that we can avoid that trap.

So what's a "public good?" In economic parlance, a pure "public good" is something that is both "non-rival" and "non-excludable."

"Non-rival" means that one person's usage of the thing doesn't diminish another person's use of it, and "non-excludable" means that there's no way anyone can keep someone else from benefiting from it once it is out there. Common examples include a fireworks display, national defense, and clean air. The HG Theorem doesn't claim to apply to other forms of public spending, such as mass transit, which are both excludable and rival to some degree. (Transit has a capacity limit, and even if we've abolished racially discriminatory Jim Crow laws, the fact that they were even possible proves excludability.)

Nevertheless, there's strong evidence that public spending on goods other than "pure public goods" raises land selling values too, just perhaps not to the same degree (Shankar, Young, Haas, & Esling, 2019). I contacted Nicolaus Tideman, who tells me that a variant of the HG Theorem for non-pure-public-goods holds that "the combination of land value increases and charges equal to marginal cost will finance these expenditures."

However, "neither theorem applies if people have different tastes or if benefits do not decline with distance." I think what he's saying is that most public works can be funded entirely by the increases in land rental value they generate, supplemented with modest user fees. I also think he's saying it depends on what kind of public work it is. If you spend public money on a truly hideous art installation that only three people like, that's not going to raise land prices. If your public work is of equal benefit to everybody no matter where they live (such as clean air or national defense), that's also not going to raise the price of land, because no location benefits from it more than any other.

If you put ATCOR, the Henry George Theorem, and observations about non-pure-public-goods-spending together, one could postulate a virtuous cycle where government investment is always able to pay for itself without creating a drag on the economy and *without* any deficit spending or debt.

Even if we don't count on any of those effects, the above figures are already pretty astounding, even using the pessimistic Federal Reserve figures at the lower capitalization rate.

If you want to see someone much smarter than I put all this together into an actual policy paper that proposes a modest Land Value Tax to boost the economy, abolish the income tax, *and* balance the budget, check out the paper Nicolaus Tideman sent me: *Post-Corona Balanced-Budget Super-Stimulus: The Case for Shifting Taxes Onto Land* (co-written with Kumhof, Hudson, and Goodhart).

And in case you're wondering who Nicolaus Tideman is, here's a quick bio from his Wikipedia Page:

> *Tideman was an Assistant Professor of Economics at Harvard University from 1969-1973, during which time from 1970-1971 he was a Senior Staff*

Economist for the President's Council of Economic Advisors. Since 1973 he has been at Virginia Tech, with various visiting positions at Harvard's Kennedy School of Government (1979-1980), University of Buckingham (1985-1986), and the American Institute for Economic Research (1999-2000).

We can quibble about the estimation methods and the cap rates, but by George, land rents represent a huge amount of value. If nothing else, a high LVT could offset many unpopular and inefficient taxes without cutting the budget, or it could be used to fund important programs we supposedly can't currently afford.

CONCLUSION:
America's land rents are, in fact, equal to a sizable percentage of the annual budget.

Ironically, by demonstrating that land taxes can raise a large amount of money, I may actually have set up another type of criticism; land taxes don't raise too *little* revenue, they raise *too much.* This critique is mostly made on moral/ideological grounds and typically comes from the right—to which I'll just let arch-conservative William F. Buckley (apparently both a Georgist *and* a full-on Single-Taxer) make the case (Buckley, 2000):

> *CALLER: I've heard you describe yourself as a Georgist, follower of Henry George, but I haven't heard much in having you promote Land Value Taxation and his theories and I'm wondering why that is the case.*

BUCKLEY: It's mostly because I'm beaten down by my right-wing theorist and intellectual friends, they always find something wrong with a single tax idea. What I'm talking about this man, Henry George, who said, look, there's infinite capacity to increase capital and to increase labor, but none to increase land. And since wealth is a function of how they play against each other, land should be thought of as common property.

The effect of this would be that if you have a parking lot and the Empire State Building next to it, the tax on the parking lot should be the same as the tax on the Empire State Building because you shouldn't encourage land speculation.

Anyways, I've run into tons of situations where I think the single tax theory would be applicable. We should remember also this about Henry George: he was sort of co-opted by the Socialists in the twenties and the thirties but he was not one at all. Albert J Knox, a book on him makes that plain. Plus—also he believes in only that tax, he believed in zero income tax.

At the end of the day, you either accept the moral arguments for making land rental value common property or you don't. If Buckley's argument that "a parking lot next to the Empire State building should be in principle taxed at the same rate as the skyscraper" doesn't sit right with you, I'm not sure appealing to empirics is going to convince you, as the disagreement likely comes from a much more fundamental place.

Mind you, if you think all taxation is theft, well, Land Value Tax is a tax, so presumably you have a problem with it on those grounds. However, if you accept that you live in a society that must, at least occasionally, tax things, you might opt for what Milton Friedman called "the least bad tax" (Friedman, 1978):

> *AUDIENCE MEMBER: Dr. Friedman, my name's Ed Arten, I'm in free enterprise, I feel and—I find the income tax totally antagonistic to true free enterprise. Can we run the country without income tax?*

> *FRIEDMAN: Well, there's a sense in which all taxes are antagonistic to free enterprise. And yet, we need taxes. We have to recognize that we mustn't hope for a utopia that is unattainable. I would like a great deal less government activity than we have now, but, I do not believe we can have a situation where we don't need government at all.*

> *We do need to provide for certain essential government functions. The police function, the national defense function, function of preserving law and order, maintaining a judiciary.*

> *So, the question is, which are the least bad taxes? And in my opinion—and this may come as a shock to some of you—the least bad tax, is a property tax on*

the unimproved value of land, the Henry George
argument of many many years ago.

16

Bank Loans and Land

So, we've established that land is responsible for the bulk of urban real estate values (and urban real estate values are the bulk of total real estate values), and land rents are large enough to make a big dent in any budget. Now, let's look at something that affects everyone: the share of land value represented in bank loans.

Banks exist for at least two stated purposes—to give people a safe place to store their money and to provide capital in the form of loans to people engaged in productive activities. There's a song from *Mary Poppins* where a group of bankers enthusiastically tell a young child that investing his money in the bank will support ambitious infrastructure projects such as "Railways through Africa! Dams across the Nile! Fleets of ocean greyhounds! Majestic, self-amortizing canals!" (Stevenson R., 1965). That song is a pretty good summary of the Econ 101 story we're told about what banks do with their depositors' money.

Banking is obviously way more complicated than "you give the bank your money and then they lend it out to people," what with fractional reserve banking, the Federal Reserve, and all the rest of it. However, we don't really care about that side of things for the purposes of this question. All we want to know is *given that banks have money, what do they do with it?* Lately, they lend it out to people who want to buy real estate, according to *The Great Mortgaging: Housing Finance, Crises, and Business Cycles* (Jordà, Schularick, & Taylor, 2014). This chart shows three snapshots from 1928, 1970, and 2007 of the share of all bank lending that goes to real estate for a selection of major countries around the world.

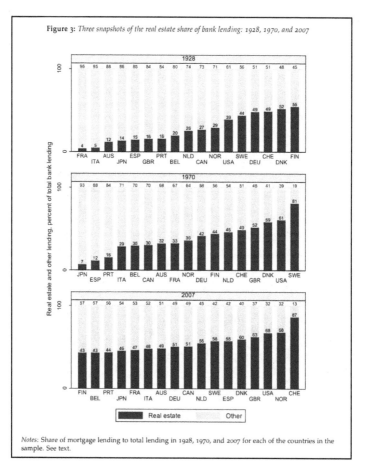

Figure 3: *Three snapshots of the real estate share of bank lending: 1928, 1970, and 2007*

Notes: Share of mortgage lending to total lending in 1928, 1970, and 2007 for each of the countries in the sample. See text.

Here's another visualization that takes all the countries together and plots it over time, going back to the late 1800's.

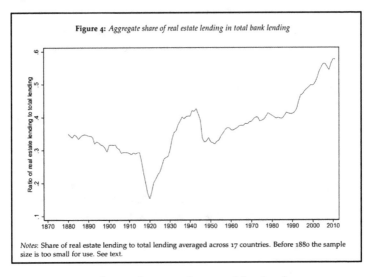

Figure 4: *Aggregate share of real estate lending in total bank lending*

Notes: Share of real estate lending to total lending averaged across 17 countries. Before 1880 the sample size is too small for use. See text.

As we can see above, this is truly a worldwide phenomenon, and it is been on a continuous upward trend since about 1950. As of today, the real estate share of bank lending has grown to nearly twice the level it was in Henry George's time.

Let's see if we can spot check some of these statistics by looking up another source. Positive Money provides this graph breaking down per-sector lending in the UK (Bikas, 2018). They give the Bank of England itself as the source for their data.

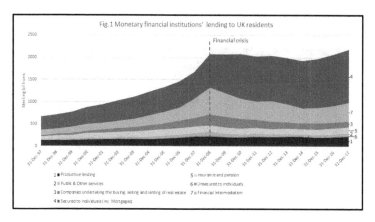

Source: Table C1.2 Bank of England statistics via Positive Money

Counting pixels and working out the percentage by hand, it looks like real estate (regions 3 and 4) combined for about 45% circa 2007 and climbed to 60% in 2017. The 2007 figures are smaller than those given in the above charts from *The Great Mortgaging* but are still huge in either case.

Is there anywhere else we can check easily? New Zealand (which isn't covered in *The Great Mortgaging*) has this really cool dashboard that breaks down all the bank loans in their country (Reserve Bank of New Zealand, 2021). As you can see, the majority of loans are for housing.

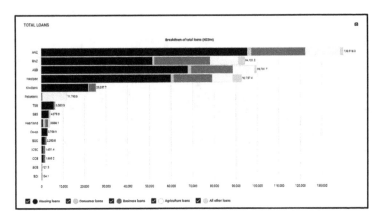

Here's another view of the same data (Vaughan, 2021):

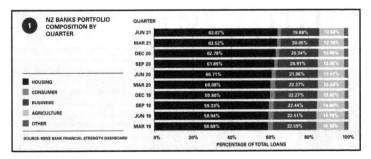

I could dig further, but I think I've seen enough to convince me of this general point. The majority of bank loans in a lot of major developed countries (including the US, UK, and New Zealand) are for real estate, and, as we've already shown, the majority of real estate's value is concentrated in land. Whether or not land represents a clear majority of bank loans, it is undeniably a big chunk.

CONCLUSION:
Land represents a large percentage of all major bank loans.

Okay, so what? Why is it such a big deal if banks spend a lot of money chasing after real estate? Although financing the construction of new houses is a good thing, none of the money tied up in the buying and selling of land is itself productive, because no new tangible wealth is created. Also, all this cheap credit for land just means more bids driving up land prices. Not only are real estate bank loans not making the economy any better, they're actively making it worse.

Anyone who lived through 2008 knows first-hand how seemingly abstract real estate investment shenanigans can come smashing into your everyday life and bring the entire world economy down with it as it did during the subprime mortgage crisis. China in particular is now grappling with many of the same problems (Stevenson & Li, 2021).

Now take a look at this eye-popping quotation from Tideman's paper, section 3.7.1, "The Financial Sector," (Tideman, Kumhof, Hudson, & Goodhart, 2021):

> *Hudson (2012, 2018) has shown that most land rent is paid out as interest to banks and that bank credit is a major driver of increases in housing prices ("real estate is worth whatever the bank will lend against it"). Further empirical support is offered by Favara and Imbs (2015), and La Cava (2015) finds that this can explain the increase in the share of housing in capital income studied by Rognlie (2015). Ryan-Collins et al. (2017) and Turner (2017) argue that a self-reinforcing cycle between bank lending and land value increases has caused a shift in bank lending from business loans to mortgages and the inflation of land prices, and*

*this has impaired financial stability, as also argued
in Keen (2017).*

That Rognlie (2015) citation is worth unpacking in particular.
Rognlie got a lot of attention for pointing out some major
flaws in Thomas Piketty's famous book, *Capital in the 21st
Century.*

Piketty's argument is that the rate of return to capital exceeds
the overall rate of economic growth, leading to wealth
concentration and inequality (Piketty, 2014). Rognlie pointed
out in his paper that Piketty was improperly handling the
depreciation of capital assets. Once you account for this, you
find the outsized returns to "capital" driving inequality are
due almost entirely to housing (Rognlie, 2015).

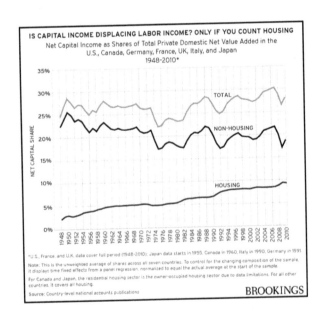

The unaffordability of housing appears to be not a mere symptom of inequality but rather a key driver of it. Banks contribute to that unaffordability by acting as the shadow rentiers of the entire economy.

17

Land and Personal Asset Holdings

Let's return to two graphs from Part I. The first shows that something like 40% of all gross personal assets in Spain represent land (Blanco, Bauluz, & Martínez-Toledano, 2018).

About 25-30% are "financial assets" that must ultimately cash out to some mixture of real assets (land and capital), so the true percentage due to land is probably higher than 40%.

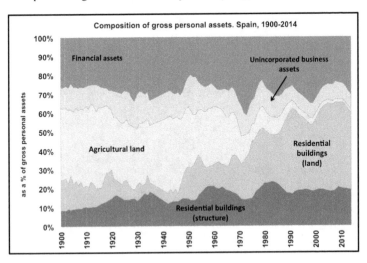

The second chart shows that about half of the value of real assets in the United Kingdom is due to land:

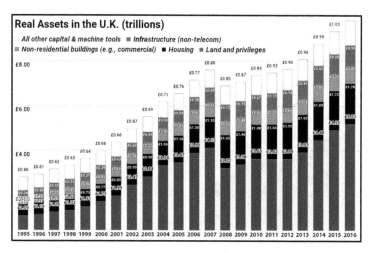

Based on data from the United Kingdom National Accounts: The Blue Book 2017. Published Oct 31, 2017. Revision Period: Beginning of each time series. Date of next release: July 2018. The "privileges" in "Land and privileges" are things like taxi medallions and patents, that were worth "almost zero" according to Nate Blair, who prepared the chart.

Next, here are two graphs from *Capital in the Twenty-First Century* breaking down "national capital" for Britain and France by sector (Piketty, 2014):

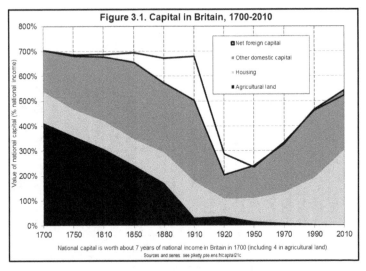

Figure 3.1. Capital in Britain, 1700-2010

National capital is worth about 7 years of national income in Britain in 1700 (including 4 in agricultural land)
Sources and series: see piketty.pse.ens.fr/capital21c

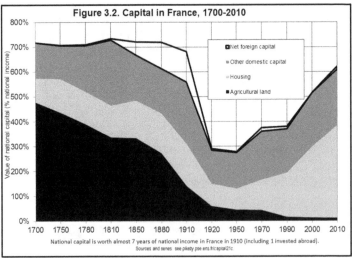

Figure 3.2. Capital in France, 1700-2010

National capital is worth almost 7 years of national income in France in 1910 (including 1 invested abroad).
Sources and series: see piketty.pse.ens.fr/capital21c

In the olden days, the majority of national capital was in agricultural land. Nowadays, the majority of it is in housing. I can work out that in 1700, about 76% of Britain's and 80% of

France's national capital was real estate. In 2010, those figures were 55% and 61%, respectively.

What about the US? Here's a figure from Tideman & co's big paper, which uses OECD[11] numbers to chart the share of household wealth in the USA due to "non-produced assets" (what Georgists call "Land": conventional land, natural resources, and everything else that isn't created by humans) (Tideman, Kumhof, Hudson, & Goodhart, 2021).

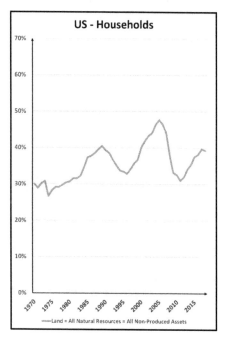

As we can see, it hovers around 40%.

---

[11] Organisation for Economic Co-operation and Development

Land represents about 40% of household assets in the USA. It also represents more than 40% of asset values in Spain and somewhere between 50-60% of asset values in the France and UK. How about the rest of the world? According to a giant report by McKinsey in 2021, real estate holdings account for two-thirds of all *global* real assets, with more than half of that coming from land (Woetzel, et al., 2021):

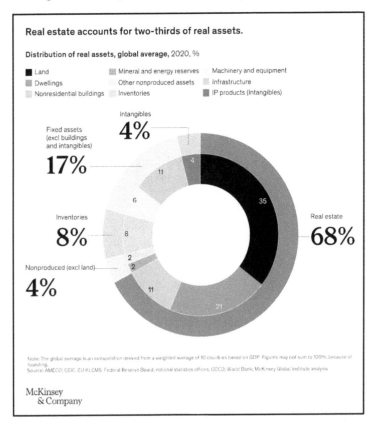

Real estate accounts for two-thirds of real assets.

Distribution of real assets, global average, 2020, %

- ■ Land
- ■ Dwellings
- ■ Nonresidential buildings
- ■ Mineral and energy reserves
- Other nonproduced assets
- ■ Inventories
- Machinery and equipment
- ■ Infrastructure
- ■ IP products (Intangibles)

Intangibles
4%

Fixed assets (excl buildings and intangibles)
17%

Inventories
8%

Nonproduced (excl land)
4%

Real estate
68%

4
11
6
35
8
2
2
11
21

Note: The global average is an extrapolation derived from a weighted average of 10 countries based on GDP. Figures may not sum to 100%, because of rounding.
Source: AMECO; CEIC; EU KLEMS; Federal Reserve Board; national statistics offices; OECD; World Bank; McKinsey Global Institute analysis

McKinsey
& Company

If you add together the 35% due to conventional land and the 4% due to "non-produced" assets (which, among other things, includes mineral and energy reserves), you get the amount represented by the Georgist definition of Land: 39% of all real assets in the entire world. That figure rises to 43% if you also count IP as "Economic Land."

That seems like a pretty big deal to me.

CONCLUSION:
Land does, in fact, represent a significant percentage of the value of gross personal assets in developed countries, including the USA.

Now some of you might be nervous at this point. Are those awful Georgists about to ruin me with LVT? I can certainly sympathize, seeing as I'm a homeowner myself. This is where I think the Citizen's Dividend (UBI) should probably come in.

Let's use $1.2 trillion in 2020, the *most pessimistic* figure for America's land rents (the Federal Reserve method at the low 5% capitalization rate). I happen to think the true value for America's land rents is closer to the more optimistic figure of $3.5 trillion (Smith's method at the 8% capitalization rate). The upshot is that if we use the $1.2 trillion figure for a generous citizen's dividend, that will probably still leave a good amount of room for also offsetting existing taxes used to fund the budget.

If we split our $1.2 trillion citizen's dividend among all ~209 million American citizens over the age of 18, then anybody sitting on a property worth less than ~$230,000 is going to either break even or turn a profit.

Property Value	Land Share	Land Value	100% LVT	Citizen's Dividend	Net Tax
$10,000	50%	$5,000	$250	$5,738.11	-$5,488
$50,000	50%	$25,000	$1,250	$5,738.11	-$4,488
$100,000	50%	$50,000	$2,500	$5,738.11	-$3,238
$200,000	50%	$100,000	$5,000	$5,738.11	-$738
$250,000	50%	$125,000	$6,250	$5,738.11	$512
$500,000	50%	$250,000	$12,500	$5,738.11	$6,762
$1,000,000	50%	$500,000	$25,000	$5,738.11	$19,262
$5,000,000	50%	$2,500,000	$125,000	$5,738.11	$119,262

This simplistic table makes a few assumptions, of course. We fix land share at 50%, and capitalization rate at 5%. But keep in mind that *every citizen* would get the dividend, so if you have two adults in your household, the table breaks even at just under $500,000 in property value.

Property Value	Land Share	Land Value	100% LVT	Citizen's Dividend	Net Tax
$10,000	50%	$5,000	$250	$11,476.22	-$11,226
$50,000	50%	$25,000	$1,250	$11,476.22	-$10,226
$100,000	50%	$50,000	$2,500	$11,476.22	-$8,976
$200,000	50%	$100,000	$5,000	$11,476.22	-$6,476
$250,000	50%	$125,000	$6,250	$11,476.22	-$5,226
$500,000	50%	$250,000	$12,500	$11,476.22	$1,024
$1,000,000	50%	$500,000	$25,000	$11,476.22	$13,524
$5,000,000	50%	$2,500,000	$125,000	$11,476.22	$113,524

This is not a recipe for bankrupting the middle class. In fact, it compensates everyone for helping make America a desirable place to live. This compensation is paid primarily by those who gatekeep the most valuable locations and natural resources, things which were not brought into existence by anyone's hard work or investment.

Also, keep in mind that LVT would see the elimination of the portion of property tax that falls on buildings. I just checked my own property tax records (I live in the suburbs of a medium-sized town far from any major urban cores). If the assessed land share more than doubled to 40%, under a 100% LVT regime I'd actually save $545.05 on my property taxes every year—and that's *without* a Citizen's Dividend.

18

Land Ownership Among the Wealthy

Bill Gates, the world's fourth richest person, owns 242,000 acres of farmland across the U.S., making him the #1 owner of private farmland in the USA (Shapiro, 2021). But that's just farmland. If you're talking about all land in the USA, Gates ranks #49. Jeff Bezos is #25, and Ted Turner is #4 (Realtors® Land Institute, 2020). Rich people own a lot of land.

What portion of total real estate values are owned by the top 1%, the top 10%, and the top 50%? Quite a lot, according to the Federal Reserve.

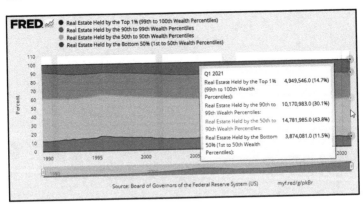

In other words, of all the real estate value in the United States, the top 1% own 14.7% of it, the top 10% own 44.8% of it, and the top 50% own 88.5% of it.

Here's how that compares against total assets:

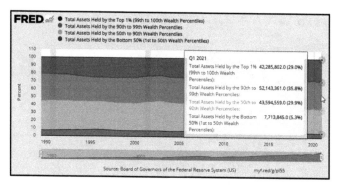

Of all asset values in the United States, the top 1% own 29% of it, the top 10% own 65% of it, and the top 50% own 94.7% of it. Compared to total asset values, it looks like real estate is a little more evenly distributed, but it is still highly stratified in an absolute sense. The top 1% own almost 15% of the country's total real estate value, and the top 10% own almost half of it. Keep in mind that it is on this basis that the top 1% and the top 10% gain the ability to collect rent from everybody else. However, where the top 1% really get their kicks is in financial assets:

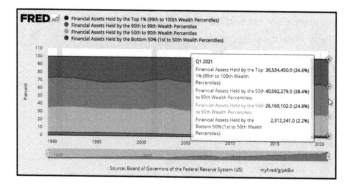

Not to mention ownership of private businesses.

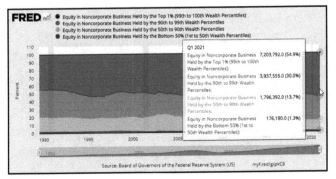

Once again, we're back to untangling the value of financial assets, which is beyond the scope of this particular investigation. In a sane world, the "ground truth" value of most financial instruments like stocks and bonds would terminate in good old-fashioned capital and labor, but we've already been through one crisis where much of the world's paper wealth turned out to be just elaborate incantations cast upon regular people's mortgages (Finra, 2021). From what we've seen about how many bank loans are tied up in real estate, we're well on our way back there.

What about sources other than the Fed? The Economist gives similarly stratified figures (The Economist, 2015) (Saez & Zucman, 2014).

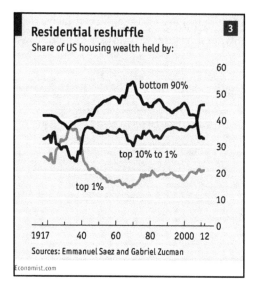

Rich people own a lot of the country's land value, and in fact, they own most of it. On top of that, housing is the world's biggest asset class (Economist, 2020). The really troubling bit is the generational gap. Every generation has lower homeownership rates than the previous one.

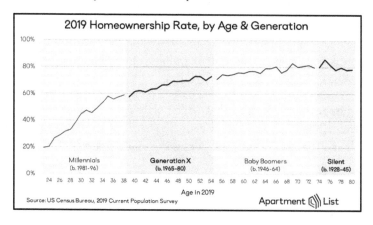

Okay, but Millennials are younger. Obviously, they have lower homeownership rates than older people. Maybe they'll catch up?

Evidence suggests they won't:

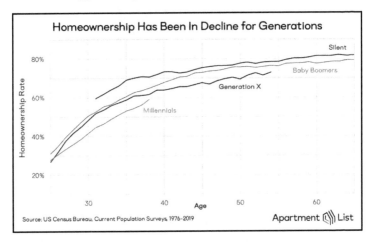

Not only is land ownership concentrated among the wealthy, it is concentrated among the *old* and wealthy. Life expectancies for the old and rich are increasing, delaying both inheritances and estate taxes past the point where it would do the next generation the most good—while they are still establishing themselves and/or trying to build families (Dahl, Kreiner, Nielsen, & Serena, 2020).

It's important to realize that Millennials are no longer young. I'm a Millennial, and I'm already 38, hardly a spring chicken. What's the picture going to look like for Zoomers?

CONCLUSION:
Land ownership is, in fact, highly concentrated among the wealthy.

We've established the following well beyond the preponderance of evidence:

☑ Most of the value of urban real estate is land

☑ USA land rents equal a large share of public spending

☑ Land represents a large share of all major bank loans

☑ Land represents a large share of all gross personal assets

☑ Land ownership is concentrated among the wealthy

BY GEORGE, LAND IS A REALLY BIG DEAL

Land is not some minor concern that only matters in pre-industrial agricultural economies. Everybody needs land, but nobody can make any more of it. You can't work, eat, sleep, or even poop without access to land (try doing any one of those things in a forbidden location and see what happens to you). The housing crisis is driven by inflated land prices, which in turn drives poverty, homelessness, and all other manner of social ills.

When we try to fix these social ills with public spending, land often soaks up and privatizes the value created by the spending. This subsidizes private actors who turn right around and use those gains to jack up everybody's rent, and the vicious cycle continues. All the while, banks continue to pour fuel on the fire.

By George, a Land Value Tax would solve this!

Part III

Is Land Value Tax
Passed on to Tenants?

19

Land Value Tax's Effect on Rents

Georgists assert that landlords cannot pass Land Value Tax (LVT) on to their tenants. (Recall that Land Value Tax is a tax on the unimproved value of land alone, excluding all the buildings and other improvements.) Many critics are skeptical of this, because just about every other tax in the world *is* passed on. Why should LVT be so special?

By George, if Land Value Tax is easily passed on to tenants, then it has no power to curb land speculation, and you can stop reading this book.

So how could a Land Value Tax *not* be passed on to tenants? We'll start by explaining the theoretical reasoning, and then we'll see if it actually plays out that way in the real world.

THEORY

Imagine I'm a landlord, and I have a vacant lot I'm renting to a tenant who's got a mobile home parked there. What's going to happen if a Land Value Tax is imposed on me? Well, I'm already charging as much as the market will bear. If I charge any more, my tenant will move out. But why shouldn't I be able to pass on a new tax to the tenant? If you tax gasoline or cigarettes, the prices go up and are ultimately borne by the customer. Why should land be any different?

The difference is that the supply of gasoline and cigarettes fluctuates, because you can produce more or less of them. When you put a tax on gasoline or cigarettes of even a few cents, somewhere in the economy there is a marginal oil well or a marginal tobacco farm whose profit margin was the same as or less than the tax. Now their profit is entirely wiped out, so what's the point of producing any more? Price signals from the market are telling producers, manufacturers, farmers, and the like, to stop producing and do something else. After all, the price is ultimately driven by supply and demand, not the wishes of a seller. Even a dedicated cartel like OPEC[12] can't enforce high oil prices by fiat. They do it by cutting off production and driving down the global supply of oil until people are forced to pay the price OPEC wants.

Okay, let's go back to land. How does Land Value Tax drive down land prices? The important thing to keep in mind is that land selling value (purchase price) is a *stock,* but land income (rent) is a *flow.* The amount of water flowing out of my tap is a flow; the amount of water currently sitting in my bathtub is a stock. The key thing is that land income drives land price and not the other way around. If a property is capable of generating $10,000 per year in rents, then the amount I'm willing to pay to buy it is $10,000 times X, where X represents how many years I'm willing to wait to break even on my investment.

How does an LVT affect the price of land? Using the bathtub metaphor again, let's put a valve under the tap, so half of the

---

[12] Oil Producing and Exporting Countries, an international oil cartel dominated by Saudi Arabia

water goes into the tub and half goes somewhere else. The amount of water flowing *out* of the tap does not change (the land is as productive as it ever was). However, the amount of water collected in my bathtub *does* change; five minutes of flow will produce less water in the tub than it did before. If I'm trying to sell my land to someone, they're going to notice the tax and correctly calculate that it will earn them half as much income over X years, so they'll pay half as much for it.

And what about rental price? The rental price comes directly from the flow. The land is in demand because of its inherent productivity; someone who occupies that land can generate a certain amount of wealth each month. Without a Land Value Tax, the owner of that land can charge rent up to the difference between their land's productivity and the best freely available alternative, establishing the "margin of productivity." This means that as productivity rises, so does the rent. (This is Ricardo's Law of Rent).

With a Land Value Tax, the owner has to pay that tax every month whether they have a tenant or not. They're already charging the highest amount the market will bear, and as we've already shown, they are unable to change the supply of land. With a fixed supply, and unchanged demand, the price tenants are willing to pay remains unchanged too, which means a tenant will move out if their landlord raises the rent. This ultimately forces the landlord to eat the tax. The price to buy the land goes down, the price for a tenant to rent it goes down, but the total amount of income the land itself produces ("land rent") stays the same. A portion of it is just being collected by the taxing agency.

That's the theory at least. Does it hold up in real life? According to the evidence, the answer is yes.

EMPIRICS

Let's try to envision what it would take to test this. Imagine a hypothetical country with a decent property assessment scheme already in place. Land and improvements are assessed separately to an objective and equalized standard, and each is taxed at a separate rate. Let's further say that this country's assessments are widely considered to be fair and well-tested against market values. As a starting condition, each of the counties in this country has its own independent land tax rate. Then, for our experimental intervention, we'll have all of the counties raise or lower the tax rate on land rental values randomly within a predefined range, all at the same time. Then we'll observe what happens to land prices.

Unfortunately for us, countries with the necessary prerequisite assessment policy are few and far between, and sovereign states don't typically run randomly controlled economic experiments on their population, so I'm afraid—wait, something almost *exactly* like this happened in Denmark in 2007.

20

The Danish Paper

What happened in Denmark was an accident, but you'd be hard pressed to design a better experimental setup if you tried. A working paper entitled "Land Taxes and Housing Prices," published at the Danish Secretariat of Economic Councils, has the full story (Høj, Jørgensen, & Schou, 2017).

One day, Denmark decided to redraw all its municipal boundaries. Regions that had been under one local government woke up the next day under a different one, immediately adopting a new set of local regulations and rules, including changed tax rates. This caused a large-scale, semi-random shuffling of Land Value Tax rates overnight.

Crucially, tax assessment *policy* was pretty much uniform throughout the country. The only thing this shakeup changed with regard to land policy was the actual individual rates of tax on land, set by the local governments. This gives us a nice big N of 250 individual areas, each with a clear before and after change in land tax rate. All of these changes came into being at exactly the same time from a single swift outside intervention, and the overall change in aggregate tax rate was close to zero:

Table 1, Average* change in land tax rates in areas				
	Areas	Tax rate before	Tax rate after	Change in tax rate
	Number	------------------ Per mille ------------------		
Increase	139	20.6	24.0	3.4
Unchanged	6	28.0	28.0	0
Decreased	105	26.1	23.5	-2.6
Total	250	23.1	23.9	0.8
Note: *Unweighted average over areas.				

(Note the "per mille"—20.6 per mille is 2.6 per cent, etc.)

The most important thing to note is that the paper's authors claim to get around the "endogeneity problem." For those of you who aren't researchers, an *endogenous* factor is something that originates from *inside* of the system you're studying, whereas an *exogenous* factor is something that originates from *outside* of it. The "endogeneity problem" is a particularly annoying gremlin that makes it hard to study economics empirically. You can never be sure that the effects you're measuring were actually caused by the intervention you're studying. Everything's a big bowl of soup, and it is hard to untangle what causes what.

Here's an example. Let's say I'm the sovereign Emperor of planet Lars. Among my many powers and privileges is the sole right to set the prime interest rate for the entire Lartian economy. One fine Tuesday, I stroll into my throne room and pull the gilded lever that changes the rate from 1.5% to 1.2%. PhD students rejoice—what a great natural experiment for measuring the effects of changes to the prime interest rate!

Well, except for the pesky fact that sovereign Emperors of planets named after themselves don't tend to just pull the prime interest rate lever for no reason. Maybe I pulled it because the economy was slowing down, or to distract everyone from the unpopular war against the Earthlings I'm currently losing. Were those effects the PhD students observed after I pulled the lever actually caused by me lowering the prime interest rate? Or were they caused by the very forces that drove me to pull the lever in the first place? What researchers really like to see is an *exogenous* effect, something that is unambiguously external to the system.

Going back to planet Lars, one day a ghostly hyperspace beast shows up, instantly eats every car on the entire planet that has a manual transmission, then vanishes in a puff of purple smoke. There's no way this had anything to do with mysterious epicycles within the Lartian economy. It was a pure exogenous shock, and we can be confident that any subsequent observed changes in the economy had something to do with the beast's insatiable appetite for stick shifts, especially if the beast was kind enough to leave a few randomly selected areas untouched as a control group. Høj, Jørgensen, and Schou claim the Danish study is the first study of Land Value Tax to enjoy such a clear exogenous trigger:

> *The method used in the present study is inspired by Borge & Rattsø (2014) who study capitalization of Norwegian property taxes during 1995-97. They also find evidence of complete capitalization. As the authors note themselves, however, examining the relationship between tax rate and house price changes may generally result in endogeneity problems, which they try to avoid using various instrumental variables. The present study is immune to this problem because the Danish local-government reform of 2007 exogenously imposes the tax rate changes.*

Although the change came from the Danish government, it had nothing to do with tax policy. They were just reorganizing the municipal map, and changes in tax rates were simply the result of whatever jurisdiction an area found itself belonging to the next day. As a quick example, if an area raised land taxes because they needed more money, the fact that the area needed more money could be just as plausible a cause for any observed changes as the change to the land tax rate. But if you change *everyone's* land taxes overnight in semi-random directions with no particular regard for the local economic or political situation, you can be more confident that subsequent changes you observe do in fact stem from that intervention.

The authors measure the before-and-after changes, apply a bunch of econometric tests, run it with and without controls just to be sure, and conclude that a Land Value Tax is "fully capitalized" into the price of the property itself. "Fully capitalized" is a fancy way of saying that the price of land goes down proportionately to how much land income is taxed away.

> The results demonstrate a clear effect on sales prices of the observed changes in land tax rates. Furthermore, the magnitude of the changes implies full capitalization of the present value of the change in future tax payments for a discount rate of 2.3 per cent, which is within the range of reasonable discount rates for households during the period in question. The analysis consequently supports the hypothesis that perceived permanent land tax changes should be capitalized fully into the price of land and property.

This just means that if you tax land rent, absent any other interventions, the selling price of land goes down. The rental income of the land available to the landlord goes down too, which means the landlord is eating the tax and can't pass it on to the tenant. If the landlord could successfully pass on the tax, we wouldn't see a decrease in the price of land that amounts to "full capitalization."

21

A Bunch of Other Studies

Now, as the saying goes, "beware the man of one study" (Alexander, 2014). It's always possible that the Danish study is a fluke or isn't representative for some reason. If the effect is real we should see it borne out repeatedly throughout the literature.

Høj, Jørgensen, and Schou cite five other prior studies they claim support their findings: Oates, 1969; Borge & Rattsø, 2014; Capozza, Green, & Hendershott, 1996; Palmon & Smith, 1998; and Hilber, 2017.

All of these studies support the same conclusion but are not as well controlled and have to do various fancy tests to deal with endogeneity. The Danish study seems like a capstone that replicates the findings of a string of prior studies and puts to rest lingering doubts about endogeneity. If we take the authors' literature review at face value, it would be a robust finding for the full capitalization hypothesis.

Let's be thorough, however. It's possible these supporting studies are misrepresented, so I looked them up and checked, just in case. They all find strong capitalization of land and property taxes into property values, and all discussed the endogeneity problem and their attempts to account for it. The studies are represented faithfully by the Danish paper and support the same conclusions. Furthermore, four of them are empirical rather than theoretical. These findings are not just the result of models and formulas, but actual real-world observations.

That still leaves the possibility that the Danish authors cherry-picked their supporting studies and ignored everyone who found the opposite conclusions, so I tried to see what a general search for research papers on this subject would turn up and if any papers would *not* support full capitalization of Land Value Taxes into property prices. Searching Google Scholar for property tax and Land Value Tax capitalization effects, I found nine additional papers.

SUPPORTING:

Bourassa studies a Land Value Tax system in Pittsburgh and finds that:

> *The incentive effect is significant but the liquidity effect is not. The incentive effect is found to encourage increases in the number of new units constructed in Pittsburgh rather than increases in the average cost of new units. (Bourassa, 1987)*

Skarburskis concludes:

> *Tilting tax rates to favor improvements at the expense of land increase the intensity of land development when all other factors are held constant. The policy can increase land values when it is applied to a small portion of a housing market and can reduce land values when applied across the entire housing market. (Skaburskis, 1995)*

Roakes says,

> *The evidence verifies that tax capitalization appears to be occurring, but does not clearly determine the resulting price outcome. Land prices increased with a decrease in real property taxes. They also appeared to increase as a result of the tax abatement system. Land prices were determined to decrease as a result of higher land taxes. (Roakes, 1996)*

Buettner finds,

> *Land taxes do capitalize into land values, whereas the monthly rent level remains unaffected by the land tax. In addition, the results point to significant spillovers from amenities and the provision of public goods across municipalities. (Buettner, 2003)*

Plummer finds,

> *If a LVT causes a property's future tax payments to increase, then the property's market value will decrease... On the other hand, if a LVT causes a property's taxes to decrease, the property's market value will increase. (Plummer, 2010)*

Plummer also notes that the capitalization effects depend on the frequency of reassessments (more frequent assessments = higher capitalization).

Choi & Sjoquist find,

> *That a revenue-neutral switch from a capital value property tax to a LVT, or a split-rate tax, results in a reduction in land rent and the tax exclusive price*

> *of housing. We find that the land rent gradient becomes flatter while the population density and housing capital gradients become steeper. (Choi & Sjoquist, 2015)*

Mills has an interesting study, titled "The Non-Neutrality of Land Value Taxation," and frames itself in opposition to LVT. It's a theoretical paper rather than an empirical one and makes a curious claim:

> *It is true that a (less than 100 percent) tax on land income is neutral, but this does not extend necessarily to a tax on capitalized land value, or changes therein. The reason is that the discounted sum of payments with the latter tax is not invariant to the intertemporal characteristics of the income stream produced by land. Among options with equal present value, it is greater for income streams skewed to the distant future than for those skewed to the near future. (Mills, 1981)*

Mills seems to be arguing that if a piece of land is subject to LVT, people will be willing to pay less to buy it, since it generates less rental income. This sounds like a full capitalization argument to me, which Mills apparently thinks is a bad thing. Regardless of how he feels about it, though, he's arguing that it *happens*, ironically putting this paper in the "support" column.

MIXED:

King doesn't have a knock-down argument for or against the full capitalization hypothesis, except to point out some quibbles with the analysis methods used in prior studies (including Oates, the seminal paper). King concludes, "our knowledge of the extent of tax capitalization is very much less than is commonly supposed." (King, 1977) One would hope King would have been more impressed by all of the studies that have come out since.

OPPOSED:

I found one study in Google Scholar that clearly and confidently rejects the hypothesis that LVT is fully capitalized into land prices.

Wyatt asserts: "It is found that LVT would increase, not lower land prices and would provide only a small incentive to building construction." (Wyatt, 1994) Wyatt relies on his own arguments paired with a literature review, which he asserts finds "no evidence" for the claims of LVT proponents.

This is strange, because Oates 1969 contradicts this and is included in Wyatt's bibliography, though I can't find a citation of Oates in the text itself. I also found Mills 1981 in his bibliography but not in the text as a citation. He does cite Bourassa 1987, which he interprets as inconclusive. He cites none of the other studies mentioned above, given they hadn't been published yet. Wyatt offers no new empirical evidence of his own, but he does cite a bunch of other papers I hadn't seen before. The majority are from the 70's and 80's, with only two as recent as the 90's, the latest one from 1991.

Since Wyatt was the only emphatically critical paper I could find on the specific subject of Land Value Tax (not property tax) capitalization into land prices, it is worth unpacking the citations that back up his arguments to see if they check out. In his introduction, he says:

> *The Valuer General of New Zealand said, "There was no evidence that the tax would (1) control urban sprawl and speculation in land; (2) encourage the construction of 'better' buildings; (3) encourage growth; or (4) cause slums to disappear"*

The source he cites is Donald Hagman's 1965 piece in the UCLA Law Review, *The Single Tax and Land Use Planning: Henry George Updated*, which took me a long time to track down. This turns out to be—and I am absolutely not kidding about this—an authorial self-insert fan fiction piece, set *in space*, that confidently expounds upon how a fictional future LVT experiment failed on the planet Mars. (Hagman D., 1964-1965)

The text Wyatt quotes comes from the mouth of a fictional character from the future. Even if we grant maximum charity that the character is referencing actual historical evidence from New Zealand from our own timeline, it comes across as confusing and muddled. Nevertheless, we can conclude four things:

1. Hagman does indeed support Wyatt's conclusion! Wyatt is not jerking our chain.

2. We don't know what went wrong with LVT in (non-fictional) New Zealand.

3. Hagman's fictional space characters from the future tell
    us nothing about whether land taxes are capitalized into
    land prices or not.

4. In the event that your space economist fan fiction is
    rejected by your favorite science fiction magazine, you
    would be well advised to try your luck with the UCLA
    Law Review instead.

This is such a bizarre article to cite as evidence in favor of
one's point that I'm going to give Wyatt a mulligan on it and
find a less strange article of Hagman's to serve as testimony
concerning the New Zealand situation.

Digging around I found a chapter from the 1978 book
*Windfalls for Wipeouts: Land Value Capture and
Compensation* (Hagman D. G., 1978), posted to
Cooperative-Individualism.org, an old school Georgist site.
There, Hagman says that when the income tax was first
introduced in New Zealand in the 1890's, Land Value Tax
was responsible for 75.7% of the combined tax yield of land +
income taxes, but over the course of the next century that
figure dropped all the way to 0.5% in 1965 and 0.3% in 1970
(note the placement of the decimal point).

Hagman isn't clear on why this is. Did land become less
important, were assessments depressed, did the land tax rate
just go down? What he does say is that various exemptions
were put into effect and that New Zealand made some moves
away from market-based valuations. Did LVT simply not
work as of 1978, or was this particular implementation
hobbled?

We've already shown in Part I that it can't be that land's importance in the economy has declined since the 19th century. Concerning New Zealand specifically (Tideman, Kumhof, Hudson, & Goodhart, 2021) says that today over half the share of non-produced assets for households is due to land.

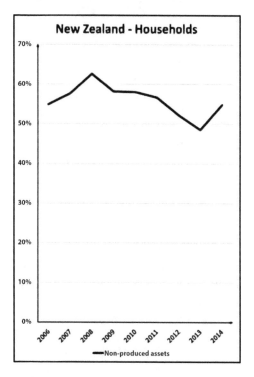

And it is worth reiterating that New Zealand banks put most of their loans towards real estate (Vaughan, 2021):

NZ BANKS PORTFOLIO COMPOSITION BY QUARTER

QUARTER	HOUSING	CONSUMER	BUSINESS	AGRICULTURE	OTHER
JUN 21	63.87%		19.88%	17.50%	
MAR 21	63.52%		20.05%	12.76%	
DEC 20	62.78%		20.34%	13.08%	
SEP 20	61.89%		20.91%	13.35%	
JUN 20	60.71%		21.90%	13.47%	
MAR 20	60.08%		22.37%	13.43%	
DEC 19	59.80%		22.27%	13.65%	
SEP 19	59.33%		22.44%	14.00%	
JUN 19	58.94%		22.51%	14.19%	
MAR 19	58.69%		22.59%	14.19%	

SOURCE: RBNZ BANK FINANCIAL STRENGTH DASHBOARD

PERCENTAGE OF TOTAL LOANS

In his case study of Australia for the same article, Hagman points to *too low* a rate of land tax as making it hard to see the full predicted effects borne out. Maybe a similar thing was going on in New Zealand?

> *It is difficult to determine whether the tax has any significant effect on land development. The tax is not high enough to have the demonstrable effects proponents of land-value taxes suggest will occur.*

In any case, the quotation from the fictional spaceman isn't particularly illuminating, and the next best source on the subject from Hagman never tell us exactly why LVT fizzled in New Zealand. What I'm *not* finding in Hagman is anything like reliable evidence that LVT is not fully capitalized into land prices.

Wyatt cites another source (Pillai, 1987) that claims that LVT hasn't worked in developing countries, but notes that the "LVT" imposed there was a flat tax based on land *acreage* rather than actual land *market value.*

Wyatt then follows up with his first solid critique—inaccurate assessments. I've just criticized plenty of official assessments in Part I, and Wyatt is absolutely correct that inaccurate assessments are a primary obstacle to successfully implementing LVT. Wyatt says: "It is noteworthy that Pennsylvania, the only state in which many cities have adopted LVT, ranks 49th out of 50 in assessment accuracy."

That's according to an old article originally published in Fortune Magazine (Breckenfeld, 1983). I don't know how Pennsylvania fares today, given it has been 39 years.

I have a whole chapter dedicated to assessment accuracy coming up next in Part IV, so let's leave that issue aside for now. What is Wyatt's argument against the full capitalization argument? Does he have any empirical data to back it up?

> *Grosskopf and Johnson also show that a revenue-neutral shift from the current property tax to a tax only on land value results in higher land prices rather than lower ones (This follows from their derivation that a uniform land and building tax decreases land prices in the long run more than a uniform land tax of equal yield).*

Okay, let's see Grosskopf and Johnson:

> *The dynamic analysis of the revenue adequacy of site value taxation is positive on the whole... The last piece of evidence available on the long-run revenue capacity of site value taxation is empirical. Site value taxation has weathered the test of time in countries all over the world. In the short run, site value taxation can indeed generate revenue equal to that of the current property tax in urban areas. (Grosskopf and Johnson, 1980)*

It seems like Grosskopf and Johnson are pro-LVT, but this isn't the question we wanted to know about. What about full capitalization?

> *In the longer run, however, untaxing buildings will cause a change in relative prices, which will in turn change the value of the tax base. Thus, by relaxing the partial equilibrium assumption that prices remain constant, we show that land prices could well increase after adjustment to change. Thus, our general equilibrium result is that the tax base could increase as a result of untaxing buildings and taxing land at a uniform rate.*

Okay, so maybe Wyatt was right?

> *Given a number of assumptions that are quite conservative, a site value tax can keep pace. Therefore, our revenue conclusion is that taxing land instead of land and buildings will not, in itself, cause cities to find themselves with financial difficulties.*

Call it a maybe? This 1980 paper cited a few empirical results, but its own conclusions largely rest on theoretical models.

Wyatt's chief argument is that the supply of land is not really fixed; the true figure should not be "all the land there is" but rather "all the land supplied to the market within a given jurisdiction," which he asserts is constantly changing. He further notes that many proponents of LVT, such as the famed Georgist Mason Gaffney, themselves admit that under certain conditions, the price of land may not change in the wake of an LVT being levied (this is due to Gaffney's ATCOR theory that any cuts in labor and capital taxes cause land rents to rise). He goes on to attack many other assumptions of the Georgist philosophy and ultimately claims that "there is no reliable evidence for the capitalization effect which proponents believe would reduce land prices." Wyatt's preferred alternative is a "progressive property tax," essentially a wealth tax. He goes on:

> *Therefore, if one allows for capitalization of higher service levels as well as higher land taxes, one may find that higher-tax areas actually attract firms and households, resulting in greater demand for land, hence higher land prices.*

This just seems like a straight-up affirmation that a weak form of the Henry George theorem is true.

> *It is likely a higher tax on land would be accompanied by greater spending on services which would add to the value of land. As is well documented, the major source of land value derives from public improvements (Czamanski 1966)*

Okay, now we're getting somewhere! LVT proponents claim that an LVT can't be passed on to tenants, but Wyatt is saying that if you turn around and spend that LVT money on making your city better and more desirable, then the increased demand for land in your city might more than offset the negative capitalization of the tax into the sales price of land. That's a solid argument. Notice that Wyatt is here implicitly admitting to capitalization of land taxes into land prices; he's just *also* arguing that there are other effects in

play. What Wyatt doesn't realize is that the natural policy
conclusion here is . . . a 100% LVT that recaptures all the
added gains to land value from public spending. He doesn't
provide his own empirical study to back up his claims, mind
you. He does, however, cite Mary Edwards' 1984 study and
claims it says an Australian LVT had no effect on housing
prices, once you control for public expenditure level.

What does Edwards have to say?

> *Given both the tax levels of local governments (or*
> *expenditure levels) and the site tax variable ... it is*
> *difficult to conclude if either has an effect due to*
> *multicollinearity. When one omits the local*
> *expenditure level, the site tax variable is very great*
> *and extremely significant with respect to the*
> *average value of new houses. (Equation [5])*
>
> *After the inefficiencies of autocorrelation are*
> *removed in Equation [9], the level of taxation has a*
> *decreasing effect on the stock of dwellings but the*
> *greater the proportion of communities that tax the*
> *unimproved capital value of land in each state, the*
> *greater the growth in housing stock.*
>
> *The results of this paper coincide with the*
> *conclusions of A. R. Hutchinson—that not taxing*
> *improvements tends to bring about an increase in*
> *the average value of housing and the value of total*
> *housing stock. (Edwards, 1984)*

I see what Wyatt is saying, but it feels like another
misrepresentation. Maybe Edwards' study by itself doesn't
have a strong enough result to untangle the effects of site

value tax from public spending levels, but to frame it as if Edwards herself is saying there's no evidence for LVT feels like putting words in her mouth. Worse, Wyatt doesn't address the part where she *does* try to deal with autocorrelation and finds the tax still has a beneficial effect.

In 1994, I might have found Wyatt's argument compelling, but a bunch of his sources don't seem to be saying quite what he thinks they do. When they do support his claims, they're largely old and non-empirical (or from outer space).

I've just read thirteen other papers that provide plenty of empirical evidence from multiple case studies all over the world, culminating in the Danish study. We can further add to that all the long-standing theoretical arguments in LVT's favor, as well as all the prominent economists from competing and outright hostile schools such as Milton Friedman, Friedrich Hayek, Marx & Engels, and Paul Krugman who have either advocated for some form of LVT themselves or openly acknowledged it as the "least bad" tax (Friedman, 1978), (Moore, 2017), (Hayek, 1960) (Engels & Marx, 1848).

This is really strong evidence for the full capitalization hypothesis, the natural corollary to which is that landlords can't pass on Land Value Tax.

CONCLUSION:
Land Value Tax can't be passed on to tenants.

There is one thing Wyatt had a point about, however:

The real underlying issue here may be to correct
the systematic underassessment of the value of land
rather than to introduce a higher nominal tax rate
on land.

If land is truly chronically underassessed, then simply making land assessments more accurate across the board will give you a similar effect to raising the rate of LVT, without touching the nominal tax rate or changing any laws.

This is because every property tax has a partial Land Value Tax hidden inside. The portion of the property tax that falls on buildings is bad because it incurs deadweight loss, but the portion that falls on land is an LVT and is good. Just by raising land assessments close to their true value, you are effectively increasing the rate of the hidden LVT, without increasing the amount of tax that falls on buildings.

This falls well short of 100% LVT, and leaves the harmful tax on improvements untouched, but it is an incremental improvement that can be done right now, entirely within the existing political structure. Georgism predicts that partial LVT will have partial benefits, and all you have to do is improve the practice of assessments.

There are two ways land can be chronically underassessed. The first is when the assessed value of the property is way below market value, and the primary deficit is because the land selling value is underestimated. This isn't uncommon in big cities in the midst of housing crises.

	TOTAL VALUE	LAND VALUE	PROPERTY TAX RATE	TAX ON BUILDINGS	TAX ON LAND	LAND TAX RATE
Underassessed	100,000	10,000	2%	1,800	200	0.20%
Corrected	140,000	50,000	2%	1,800	1,000	0.71 %

In this example, raising the assessed value of land to its true value more than triples the effective rate of the hidden land tax, *without* raising the amount of tax on the building.

The second way land can be chronically underassessed is when the total value of the property is properly assessed close to market value, but the value of the land is understated relative to the building. This often happens with the "cost approach" method we discussed in Part II. If you just improve the land assessment, you *shift* the tax burden off of the building and on to the land.

	TOTAL VALUE	LAND VALUE	PROPERTY TAX RATE	TAX ON BUILDINGS	TAX ON LAND	LAND TAX RATE
Underassessed	100,000	10,000	2%	1,800	200	0.20%
Corrected	100,000	50,000	2%	1,000	1,000	1.00 %

Okay, but in this second chart isn't the owner paying $2,000 no matter what? Why would they care what the tax internally "falls" on so long as the topline figure is the same?

There are a couple of reasons. For one, although it won't have any immediate effect on an individual whose total property value doesn't change, for many people it *will* change. Some will go up, some will go down, and the resulting taxes will encourage putting land to its highest and best use. And for those whose property values don't change at all, now there is no disincentive to build further improvements. Build a big multifamily unit? Remodel your bathroom? Build a nice big building downtown that supplies lots of jobs or housing? Go nuts, you won't be punished for it with increased taxes.

Ideally, the next step after shifting taxes from buildings to land is to abolish the portion of the tax that falls on buildings.

This leads directly to our next question, and the last and greatest objection to Georgism: can we actually perform accurate assessments that meaningfully and cleanly separate land value from improvements, such as buildings?

Part IV

Can Land Value
Be Accurately Assessed?

22

The Basics of Assessment

Okay, so land is a really big deal, and it looks like Land Value Tax can't just be passed on to tenants, which means Georgism works great in theory. But in order to implement it effectively, you need to be able to price all the land parcels, accurately. Or at least accurately *enough*. So, how do you actually do that?

Some friends suggested I get in touch with Ted Gwartney, former professor of Real Estate Appraisal at Baruch College, New York. He has an MAI in Land & Commercial Appraisal from the Appraisal Institute and is former president of the Council of Georgist Organizations. He has a lot of professional experience as an assessor in British Columbia, Southfield in Michigan, and Hartford, Bridgeport, and Greenwich in Connecticut.

He was even a co-signer of a famous open letter to Gorbachev in 1990 urging the Soviet premier to establish a Land Value Tax to provide a stable basis for the new economy as Russia struggled to rise from the collapse of communism (Tideman, Open Letter to Mikhail Gorbachev, 1990). Other co-signers included four Nobel Laureates: Franco Modigliani, Robert Solow, James Tobin, and William Vickrey, not to mention William Baumol of Baumol's Cost Disease (Alexander, Considerations on Cost Disease, 2017). Unfortunately, the Russian authorities went with Harvard

Professor Jeffrey Sachs' "shock therapy" instead (Wedel, 1998), and the rest is history, as anyone who lived through the post-Soviet chaos can tell you (Daley, 2020).

Ted Gwartney also gives online seminars. To prep for this section of the book, I attended his 5-week course, "Assessing Land Values—Principles and Methods" from the Henry George School of Social Science, which I'll reference throughout this piece.

Gwartney couldn't be more Georgist if he tried, so for balance, I looked up about a dozen research papers on the topic of land value assessment in Google Scholar, some of which are cited below. I also consulted the homepage of the International Association of Assessment Officers (IAAO), the international professional body for real estate assessors that sets industry standards. Then I looked up the local policies of various appraisal districts in my home state of Texas to see how things are actually done in practice in my local area.

Here's what I found.

- There are common principles that everybody, Georgist or not, seems to agree on

- Several promising new methods have come out in the last 15 years

- The actual practice in many places isn't great

- The actual practice in other places is pretty good

- We can probably improve on both the state of the art and the actual practice

- Georgists assert we're consistently undervaluing land basically everywhere

This book doesn't cover specific case studies where Georgism has been successfully tried in deep detail. That said, solid examples that uphold the purported benefits of Georgism in the wake of an LVT policy would be good evidence for accurate (enough) land assessment being feasible—"what works in practice can work in theory."

ASSESSMENT 101

Pretty much everybody agrees on the basic algebraic formula for deriving land value:

Total Value = Land Value + Improvements Value

The total selling value is whatever the property sells for. The selling value of improvements is the selling value of all of the buildings and other permanent structures and investments that sit on top of the land. The land selling value is the selling value of the location itself and any of its natural endowments. When two factors are known, you can calculate the third, which is then known as the *residual*. The high-level strategy for doing valuations thus becomes to use whatever evidence you have to get any two of these values. From there, you can simply deduce the third.

The quality of your assessments will depend not only on the method you use and the expertise of your assessment officers, but also on your local policies. The IAAO lists the following as "core principles" that local assessment policies should ideally have (IAAO, 2020):

- Assessments based on market selling values

- Frequent and regular (preferably annual) updates to assessments

- A broad tax base with limited exemptions

- Targeted, easily accessible relief programs for those who need assistance

- Well managed, transparent, and adequately funded mass appraisal procedures

Everyone is in further agreement about the three basic "approaches" to value estimation: the market approach, the cost approach, and the income approach.

THE MARKET APPROACH

This is the most common approach. You gather a bunch of information about comparable properties, look at past selling prices and rents, and make adjustments for differences. This is greatly aided by modern computerized databases, as well as Geographic Information System (GIS) mapping and visualization tools. Remember those spot checks I did in Part II to estimate the value of the land under a building in San

Francisco using a nearby, similarly-sized empty lot? That was me (crudely) using the market approach.

THE COST APPROACH

In this approach, you estimate the cost of the buildings minus depreciation. Professionals that value residential and commercial buildings often rely on something called Marshall & Swift's Valuation Service. This is a fancy calculator where you plug in all the different characteristics of your building, and it spits out a cost estimate. You can think of it as a Kelley Blue Book, but for buildings. Once you have the cost of your building, you apply certain widely-accepted depreciation formulas based on its age.

The cost approach has two chief limitations. The first is that it requires a lot of detailed information about the building. The second is that the cost to build something isn't necessarily the same as what it would sell for in today's market. Therefore, this approach tends to overestimate building values and underestimate land values, as discussed in detail in Part I.

THE INCOME APPROACH

In this approach, you look at the net income (rent - expenses) that a commercial or residential property generates and then use the prevailing capitalization rate of the area to get the property value. You typically use this formula:

Value = Income / Rate

This gives you the total property rental value, and from there, you can use one of the other two approaches to separate land rental value from building rental value. Crucially, any observed land or property tax needs to be factored into the observed "income" portion. Even if the state is collecting the tax, it is part of the flow that originates from the property, and thus affects the full untaxed market value of the property. Naively, you might expect a 100% Land Value Tax to drive itself to zero because it also drives down the purchase price of the land to approximately nothing. To avoid this, you figure out the capitalized value of the LVT that's already been applied to get the untaxed land selling value.

These are the basic methods that we've used to value properties "by hand" over the last century, and there are many who claim that these are good enough. As for separating land from buildings, Ted Gwartney prefers to estimate the value of land directly whenever possible and derive the building value as a residual. He claims it is easier to assess land than buildings, because in most cases, the value of land is derived almost entirely from the location. Land also doesn't have as many fiddly variables, like how much damage your roof took from the last hailstorm and whether you've remodeled your bathroom in the past five years.

Let's dive deeper.

23

Assessing the Assessments

Okay, so once you've made all your assessments, how do you ensure they're accurate?

You test them.

Test them against what? First, we compare assessed values to ongoing transaction data from the market. Second, we count how many property owners complain about their assessed values.

The typical way you compare yourself against market transactions are "Ratio Studies," which you can read more about in "Standard On Ratio Studies: A criterion for measuring fairness, quality, equity and accuracy" (IAAO, 2013).

As for complaints, you'd think property owners would always complain out of pure self-interest, but apparently, only a minority do, and assessors actually build in an expectation for a certain number of complaints as a chief source of feedback.

If complaints are below a certain threshold (2% according to Hefferan and Boyd, 2010), that's apparently a sign that you're doing well. During Ted Gwartney's seminar, someone asked him about what tends to drive objections (Gwartney, 2010 Revaluation in Greenwich Connecticut: Henry

George's Theories, Planning the Project and Applying
Valuation Models, 2021):

> *ATTENDEE: Can you tell us what fraction of
> property owner who request a lower assessment
> argue that their land assessment is too high?*

> *GWARTNEY: A very small number. Almost all of
> the adjustments that are made are made because of
> improvements. Most of the arguments when you
> go to an appeal is about the building, it's condition,
> or what's in it or whatever. Generally, the land is
> accepted by people, they realize it's fair by looking
> at what other parcels are assessed for and most
> people don't argue it. They might say he has a
> better view than I do or whatever, but usually [the
> objection is] because there's some physical
> difference or condition in the structure.*

If the public accepts your valuations, and new market signals
match your assessments, then they can be said to be accurate.
But how precise do they need to be? Here's Gwartney's
opinion:

> *ATTENDEE: How accurate do assessments have
> to be to get the benefits of Georgism?*

> *GWARTNEY: You have a lot of wiggle room. It
> doesn't have to be perfectly precise. The idea is to
> improve on what's already being done. You get
> immediate feedback that what you're working on is*

making good results.

(Gwartney, Understanding Assessments: Introduction to Fundamentals of Assessment and the Role of the Assessor, 2021)

This is a part I'd like to know more about. Is plus or minus 5% of the true land value "good enough?" What about 15%? Or 1%? If land is under-assessed, then we basically have the same problem as the status quo, and we're not really any worse off. But if land is over-assessed, we might drive people off of it, which is bad. It seems our main problem is not *over-assessing* the value of land.

Georgists often talk about "100% LVT," but during practical discussions, it seems that their wildest dream is just to get as high as 85%. That would leave a pretty big safety margin for not over-taxing the land, even if you over-assessed it. Here's a graph I made that illustrates this:

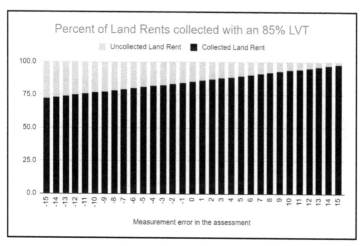

If you under-assess a property's land by 15%, the assessed value is 85% of the true value. Take 85% of that and now you're collecting 72.25% of true land rents. If you over-assess a property's land by 15%, the assessed value is 115% of the true value. If you take 85% of that, you get 97.75%. Collect all that and you're still leaving 2.25% of the true land rents on the table, but you're not going over. This is comforting, but frankly, all the evidence I've seen so far suggests that we're chronically and consistently *under*-assessing the value of land.

However, even if we can assess things accurately, it is a moot point if we can't afford to hire enough assessors to do the job thoroughly.

HOW MANY ASSESSORS DO YOU NEED?

Another critique about assessment is that you're going to need an army of property assessors peeking inside windows at all hours of the night, and that it is all going to be ruinously expensive.

Here's a slide from Gwartney's presentation, which is itself taken from an IAAO conference (Gwartney, Assessment Policy & Administration Trends: Good Government and Statewide Differences in Property Tax Assessment Practices, 2021):

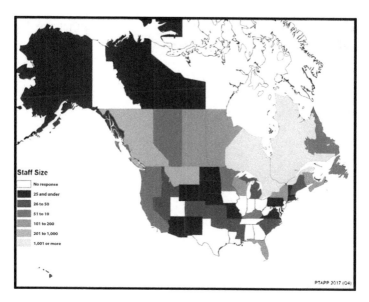

When Gwartney was assessment commissioner and chief executive officer in British Columbia, he had a staff of 690, and he says that this number has not changed significantly since then. British Columbia's population is about 5 million, so that's one assessment officer for every 7,250 British Columbians. For context, before president Biden's 2022 expansions, the IRS had a staff of 74,454, or about one IRS agent for every 4,425 Americans. I don't have data on how many property tax assessors the USA has, but the above slide suggests British Columbia's figure is on the high end.

As for how you actually do assessments, sure, you *can* send out an army of assessors to value each and every property in your jurisdiction by hand. However, not only is that labor-intensive, it is also a recipe for inconsistency. Whatever method you're using to value properties needs to be consistent and standardized across all properties, so you don't have sharp discontinuities on the assessment map that are due solely to differences between Assessor Fred and Assessor Sally's personal methodologies.

Thankfully, we're living in the modern age, and we have some fancy new tools at our disposal.

24

Modern Technology

Georgists were doing split-rate assessments to allegedly good success long before the rise of the computer, such as J. J. Pastoriza's effort in setting up a Georgist tax regime in Houston, Texas in 1912 (Pastoriza, 1915). Today, we have spreadsheets, property value databases, GIS mapping visualizations, regression analysis, machine learning. . .the works.

According to Gwartney, the Canadian province of British Columbia has revalued all its land and all its property on an annual basis, simply by using computers and market analysis, ever since he first helped them set up their system back in 1975. Not every jurisdiction revalues their land this thoroughly and this often, but Gwartney says there is no significant technical or staffing barrier standing in the way.

Gwartney has been retired for some time, so his seminar didn't cover all the latest cutting-edge techniques that have come out in the last few years. Let's look at some recent papers and see what new tools assessors have to play with.

The first on my list is "Land Value Appraisal Using Statistical Methods" (Kolbe, Schulz, Wersing, & Werwatz, 2019). This is a study on mass appraisal techniques using real estate transaction data from Berlin, Germany. It claims that not only are the results cheaper and faster to generate than those done by conventional property assessment methods, but they are also no less accurate than those done "by hand" by experts.

Kolbe et al. assert that, provided you have access to high quality market transaction data, you can perform accurate and efficient mass appraisals of land values. They chose Berlin because it "has a very effective system of property transaction data collection and storage," in contrast to other parts of Germany. They cite some prior work, "Valuation and Assessment of Immovable Property" (Almy, 2014), studying Canada, the Netherlands, and the United States, suggesting that the assessment cost per property can be brought down to €20—twenty-five times cheaper than what some other people (Fuest, Immel, Meier, & Neumeier, 2018) assert. Given an average tax receipt of €2,000 per property, this means that the assessment cost should represent only about 1% of the funds raised.

Is that good? Let's take this assertion at face value for the moment and compare it to the cost of the IRS. Federal tax receipts in 2020 were $3.42 trillion, and operation costs for the IRS were $12.3 billion (IRS, 2021), or 0.36%. However, the IRS outsources most of the labor of tax preparation to the taxpayers themselves, with compliance costs estimated between $200 billion (Bosch & Gray, 2018) and $400 billion (Erb, 2016) a year, to the delight of private tax preparation software companies like Intuit (Appelbaum, 2021). Add that up, and the total cost of federal tax collection to the economy is anywhere between 6-12% of the amount it raises. And what about sales tax? According to PriceWaterHouseCoopers (2006):

The study finds that the national average annual state and local retail sales tax compliance cost in 2003 was 3.09 percent of sales tax collected for all retailers, 13.47 percent for small retailers, 5.20 percent for medium retailers, and 2.17 percent for large retailers

A compliance cost of 1% would be way more efficient in terms of cost collection than the other two most common forms of taxation, and taxpayers don't even have to do anything themselves, other than pay the bill.

How about the accuracy? The authors cite two international examples, Australia and Lithuania, as among the few countries in the world that have both a Land Value Tax and statistical methods for mass appraisals. Hefferan & Boyd, 2010, assert that objections to assessments from property owners in Australia are less than 1%. I'm willing to buy the improved efficiency claims just by taking a look at some methodologies. It seems reasonable that computerized records and algorithms can cut costs significantly; the real question is: Are you trading off accuracy in doing so?

The other papers I found on the subject are Bencure, et al., 2019 in BayBay City, Philippines; Kilić, Rogulj, & Jajac, 2019 in Croatia; Yalpir & Unel, 2017, in Konya, Turkey; and Raslanas, et al., 2011, in Vilnius, Lithuania.

Let's dive in and examine some methods.

25

Mass Appraisal Methods

Here are some of the latest mass appraisal methods cribbed from the research papers listed above. All of these are based on taking market transaction data, plotting them out on a map, and running computations over them to estimate valuations for the properties you don't have known values for. Furthermore, all of these methods are able to value land and building values separately.

MULTIPLE REGRESSION ANALYSIS

"Use of Spatial Analysis Methods in Land Appraisal; Konya Example" (Yalipr & Unel, 2017) from Turkey gives a straightforward example of using Multiple Regression Analysis (MRA) for land valuation.

For those of you who didn't study math, let me explain regression analysis. This is a family of mathematical models where you basically take a data set and ask the question "what mathematical formula would best fit this data?" You choose a basic equation model, and then have a computer search for a set of coefficients that "best fit" that curve to the data with the least amount of error.

The simplest example is using linear regression on a scatterplot of observed data points to fit a trend line. This is a common exercise in freshman physics and statistics classes.

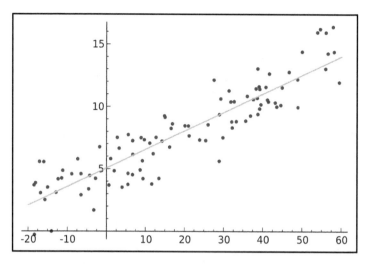

You can use more complicated versions of this numerical method to take a big bag of observations (real estate sales) and use "multiple regression" to tease out dependent variables (land value and improvements value) based on the independent variables (size, location, age, number of bedrooms) of your observations.

In this case the team identified about a hundred different factors that can affect the price of a property:

Table 1. The criteria affecting value of the land (are subheadings, written in bold and italic).

NO	A. LEGAL FEATURES	Q38	Proximity to Educational Institutions	Q78	Proximity to underpass/ overpass
Q1	Property Conditions	Q39	Proximity to Pre-schools	Q79	Proximity to Unsanitary Areas
Q2	Full Ownership	Q40	Proximity to High Schools	Q80	Proximity to was disposal areas
Q3	Shared Ownership	Q41	Proximity to Higher Education Institutions	Q81	Proximity to treatment facilities
Q4	Zoning Status	Q42	Proximity to courses	Q82	Proximity to natural gas and tube filling facilities
Q5	The Gross Floor Area	Q43	Proximity to Public Institutions	Q83	Proximity to petrol stations
Q6	Total Construction Area	Q44	Proximity to governorships	Q84	Proximity to base stations
Q7	The number of floors≥10	Q45	Proximity to Municipalities	Q85	Proximity to energy transmission lines
Q8	The number of floors<10	Q46	Proximity to Courthouse	Q86	Proximity to underdeveloped areas
Q9	Detached Building	Q47	Proximity to Jailhouse	Q87	Proximity to marsh areas
Q10	Attached Buildings	Q48	Proximity to Security Units	Q88	Proximity to natural disaster areas
Q11	Legal Restraints	Q49	Proximity to Police Stations	Q89	Proximity to not improved river areas
Q12	Right of Mortgage	Q50	Proximity to Military Zones	Q90	Proximity to Industrial Zones
Q13	Easement	Q51	Proximity to Fire Departments/ 112 Emergency	Q91	Proximity to Graveyards
Q14	Annotation of Lease	Q52	Proximity to Attraction Centers	Q92	Proximity to Worship Places
Q15	Plot Area	Q53	Proximity to Shopping Centers	Q93	Proximity to Business Centers
NO	B. PHYSICAL FEATURES	Q54	Proximity to Hypermarkets	Q94	Proximity to Parking Areas
Q16	The location of the plot	Q55	Proximity to mini-markets	Q95	The View From The Plot
Q17	Corner parcel	Q56	Proximity to open/closed bazaars	Q96	Mountain, valley, etc. views
Q18	Intermediate parcel	Q57	Proximity to commercial enterprises	Q97	Lake, river, stream, etc. view
Q19	Geometric Structure	Q58	Proximity to Cultural Centers	Q98	City view
Q20	Length of the Frontage	Q59	Proximity to cinemas/theaters	NO	D. NEIGHBOURHOOD FEATURES
Q21	The number of frontage	Q60	Proximity to historical sites and touristic attractions	Q99	Population density
Q22	Geometric shape	Q61	Proximity to Entertainment Centers	Q100	Education Level
Q23	Technical Infrastructure Services	Q62	Proximity to fairs, concert areas, etc.	Q101	Level of income
Q24	Water supply	Q63	Proximity to sport facilities	Q102	Immigrant receiving
Q25	Electricity, sewer, natural gas, and telephone	Q64	Proximity to stadium/hippodrome	Q103	Criminal Rate
Q26	Solid waste collection service	Q65	Proximity to entertainment venues	Q104	Neighborliness Relations
Q27	Storm drainage	Q66	Proximity to Green Areas	Q105	Homeowner/tenant
Q28	Unpaved road	Q67	Proximity to forest/copses	Q106	The Surrounding Environment
Q29	Asphalt road	Q68	Proximity to recreation areas	Q107	The favorite neighborhood
Q30	The Road Condition	Q69	Proximity to parks	Q108	Residential Density
Q31	The Periphery Road	Q70	Proximity to playgrounds	Q109	Development potential
Q32	Road width≥10	Q71	Proximity to Public Transportation Points	Q110	Purchasing and selling mobility of real estate
Q33	Road width<10 metre	Q72	Proximity to airports	Q111	Underground, soil, and aboveground features
Q34	The Slope of The Plot	Q73	Proximity to railway stations	Q112	Slope of the neighborhood
NO	C. LOCATIONAL FEATURES	Q74	Proximity to coach station	Q113	Geological condition
Q35	Proximity to Health Facilities	Q75	Proximity to tramway, subway and metrobus stations	Q114	Climate Condition
Q36	Proximity to health center, dispensary, etc.	Q76	Proximity to bus stops	Q115	Air Pollution
Q37	Proximity to State/Private Hospitals	Q77	Proximity to shared taxi routes	Q116	Noise Pollution

Then, you create an entry for each property, fill in the values for each of those characteristics, and run it through the regressor. Take note of how many of these factors start with the words "proximity to." Each of these can be calculated automatically just by knowing where the property is on a map, and each of them is an independent contributor to the value of the property's location.

The next step is to generate individual "index maps" that combine various related features into combined heat maps.

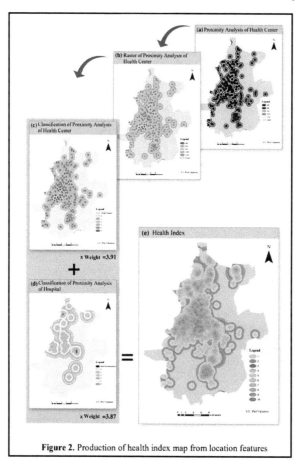

Figure 2. Production of health index map from location features

You should now have a formula into which you can plug individual property characteristics to calculate a final property value. You can get the land share of the final value by combining the contributions of all the individual factors that

you associate with "land," such as proximity to important
things.

In the verification section the authors say:

> As a result of the analysis, since the significance
> level (0.000) p <.05, corresponding to the F
> values in the ANOVA test, indicates that the
> regression analysis is appropriate and the models
> are significant. The criteria that make up the model
> account for about 85% of the market value and 15%
> cannot be explained for reasons such as economic,
> non-existent data and unearned income.

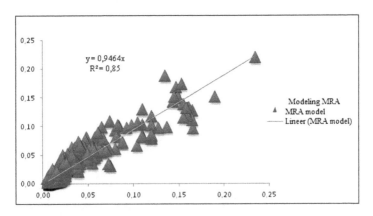

Unfortunately, they don't say anything about how accurate
their model is for assessing land values specifically.
Otherwise, this is a pretty good example of using the
Multiple Regression method for estimating the individual
contributions of various factors to overall property values.
Gwartney says Multiple Regression Analysis was a standard
method he typically used, of which this specific paper is just
one example.

NONPARAMETRIC KERNEL REGRESSION

This will be a method familiar to the programmers in the audience who have any experience with image processing algorithms. Here's an example from an article on video game development (Evans, 2021):

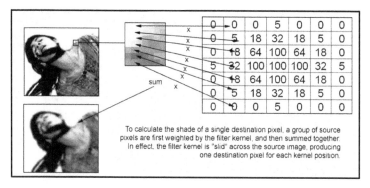

To calculate the shade of a single destination pixel, a group of source pixels are first weighted by the filter kernel, and then summed together. In effect, the filter kernel is "slid" across the source image, producing one destination pixel for each kernel position.

The basic idea here is to take a matrix of numbers, called a "kernel," and run that over every pixel in a source image. The kernel tells you how strongly to weight all of the source pixel's neighbors to compute a final result for that position. A simple "box blur" is a kernel where every value is 1 (meaning it averages the values of all neighboring pixels within a range). The more subtle gaussian blur illustrated above uses a two-dimensional normal distribution of values so that each pixel is most affected by those nearest to it.

Let's apply the same principle to land valuations. If you have a map with lots of transaction data of pure land sales—defined as sales of either vacant land or teardown properties (where the building value is essentially zero)—then you can use a special kernel filter to smoothly interpolate land values across the region.

This is a smooth curve that mostly favors close-by points, tapers off a bit, and then disregards anything outside a certain distance entirely. The big assumption here is that land values change smoothly and do not vary significantly across very short distances. There are, in fact, locations with sharp jumps in value (any town with an "other side of the tracks," for instance). However, for cases where we know a priori that land values change smoothly, this method is appropriate. No other prior restriction is placed on the form of the land value map, however, and this is why it is called "nonparametric."

Here's an illustration. The outer box is the entire search distance that the kernel considers, and the circles represent the falloff of the curve itself. The size of the box is called the "bandwidth" and is set by the user. Everything outside of it will have zero influence on the kernel's output at any given location.

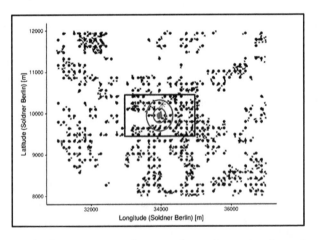

This method operates on the same basic logic that I used when I hand-estimated the land value of that San Francisco house in Part I based on the value of the empty lot next door. However, it makes the whole procedure systematic. It can easily and accurately estimate the land value of a property with a big fat building on it simply by smoothly interpolating the known values of the nearby parking lots.

Of course, it has limitations. It is a highly local operation, so if you have properties you're trying to value that don't have nearby pure land sales data, you can't really do much with this. In any case, this is just one method in your toolbox and might not be sufficient by itself. Its key advantage is that it works directly from true market data for land and doesn't need or want any other subjective data.

In the end, basic kernel estimation just fills in the land value of unmeasured locations with a local weighted average of known locations.

NONPARAMETRIC ADAPTIVE REGRESSION

Kolbe, et al. build on the kernel regression method with a technique called Adaptive Weights Smoothing (AWS), which runs in several iterations and adds additional weight to any observed data points that are sufficiently close to the point being estimated. I'm not 100% sure about what all the math means, but it seems like it is basically a "smarter" version of the basic kernel method.

SEMIPARAMETRIC REGRESSION

Kolbe, et al. go on to introduce a third method: semiparametric regression. The prior two methods assume you have plenty of "pure" land sale records to work with. However, if you're trying to work out prices in the city center, you've probably mostly got land and buildings mixed together. To do this effectively, we need more data, and this is where the "parameter" in "semiparametric" comes in.

The general model described by Kolbe et al. so far seems like a flavor of multiple regression analysis that takes the price, the location, and various characteristics of the building and feeds it into a regressor.

However, this new model is "semi" parametric. What does that mean? Well, if you already know how certain relationships between the data work a priori, it is better to enforce those relationships yourself rather than leave it to the computer. Here, we enforce the assumption that if two properties are right next to each other, then the value due to location is going to be essentially identical. This algorithm starts by ordering things geographically and then working out the differences in observed price by regressing on the difference between remaining property characteristics. In this method, the power of "location, location, location" is not something we're leaving to the regressor to discover by itself.

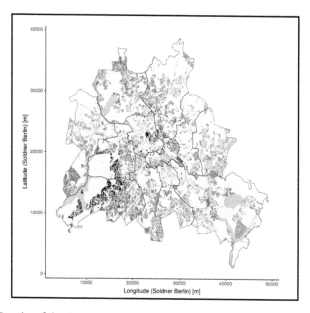

Results of the Semiparametric regression method, we can see some significant differences from the simple kernel-based model.

As you can see above, this gives you more detailed and likely more accurate results, and you're better able to assess the values of properties with buildings on them, even in the absence of pure land sales. This technique is more complicated and bakes in assumptions about the power of location, but otherwise doesn't assign subjective human weights to the various property characteristics. The chief human bias comes in the form of deciding *which* property characteristics are measured and made legible to the model in the first place.

Okay great, but how accurate are the above three methods? Their main point of comparison is this thing called the "Bodenrichtwerte," or BRW. I think that means "ground-

level-values" in English, and it is an expert-assessed map of
land values for Berlin done the traditional way.

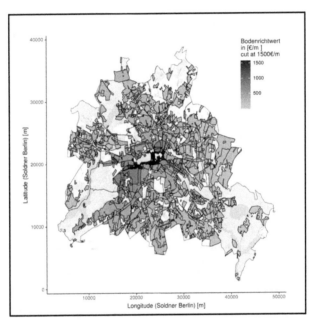

The nonparametric kernel regression method has a correlation
of 0.704 with the traditional method and has the added
disadvantage that it is not able to produce estimates for the
city center, only the outlying areas. Furthermore, the BRW
map does show sharp discontinuities, which is another knock
against the kernel method, at least for the city center.

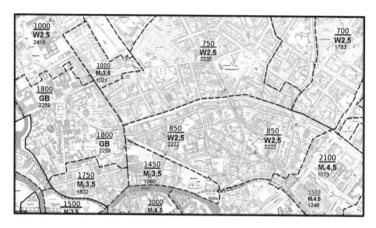

What about the iterative method? Kolbe et al. find that "the agreement between [Adaptive Weights Smoothing] land value estimates and, both, land prices and BRW land values is fairly good."

Table 1: Explanatory power. Reports coefficient of determination R^2 for bivariate regressions of BRW_i and land prices y_i on AWS land values $\hat{\theta}_i$. Regressions include a constant. Number of observations used for regressions in first row is 7,222 and 7,448 for regressions in second row.

	λ^*	λ						
	19.9	3.8415	4.4756	10.5180	16.8410	23.2840	29.7938	36.346
BRW	0.7747	0.7274	0.7390	0.7640	0.7720	0.7828	0.7733	0.7690
Land price	0.6992	0.8661	0.8526	0.7734	0.7195	0.6764	0.6525	0.6418

Doing some quick checks, their values seem to be within about 85% of the BRW values. A different Kolbe et al. paper from 2015 called "Identifying Berlin's Land Value Map Using Adaptive Weights Smoothing" goes into more detail and claims to give "similar" values to that of the BRW.

For the semiparametric method, Kolbe, et al. "found a strong
positive correlation of 0.845" between their numbers and a
previously expert-assessed set done using the traditional
method.

That sounds pretty good. It seems their margin for error is
about plus or minus 15% compared to the traditional expert
method. I'd like to see more direct comparisons against
market transactions themselves, though, because if the prior
expert assessments are wrong, then the main achievement
here is improved efficiency, not accuracy. However, this
method doesn't seem to be dramatically *less* accurate than the
old way of doing things.

The last three models came from the Berlin case study, where
you have excellent market transaction data in an extremely
wealthy and high-trust society. However, what if you're trying
to assess land in a developing nation with poor market
transaction records, weak institutions, and widespread
poverty?

INNOVATIVE LAND VALUATION MODEL (ILVM)

This is the particular name of the method described by
Bencure, et al. in their 2019 paper. They used BayBay City,
Philippines as their case study.

Whereas the previous models are very "hands-off" and let the
computer work out the relationships between prices and
property characteristics, here you get expert human opinion
directly involved in building the model, baking in weights that
directly embody judgments like "properties next to major
roads are more valuable." These judgments are based on

expert opinions that presumably come from observed experience but are a priori judgments nonetheless.

Look at this big complicated flowchart:

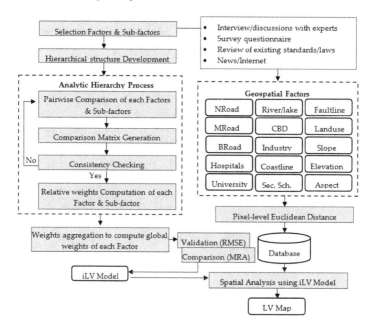

The "Analytic Hierarchy Process" in the box on the left is a particular kind of method for getting experts to set weights. The authors give this reason for using it:

> *Despite criticism pinpointed by other scholars, the AHP remains the commonly used [sic] in many research fields and practical applications. This is because the AHP: (1) overcomes human difficulty in making simultaneous judgment among factors to be considered in the model; (2) is relatively simple as compared to other MCDA [multi-criteria*

decision analysis] methods; (3) is flexible to be
integrated in various techniques such as
programming, fuzzy logic, etc.; and (4) has the
ability to check consistency in judgment

After identifying a list of "factors" that can affect land value, they group them into taxonomical buckets:

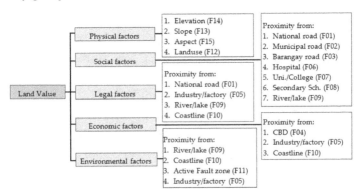

Note that certain factors like "Coastline" appear in multiple buckets; this captures the various influences a characteristic can have. For instance, land on the coast tends to be more economically valuable because of tourism, shipping, fishing, etc., so that goes under "economic." However, land that's next to the coast is also more likely to flood, so it also goes under "environmental." Then there are various land use restrictions that apply specifically to coastal areas, so it goes under "legal" as well. In this way, a single factor like "the property is on the coastline" can have both positive and negative effects on land value (e.g., it is more economically valuable but it also might flood, and there are certain things you aren't allowed to do there).

The next step is to set down some rules for how sensitive each factor is to location and distance.

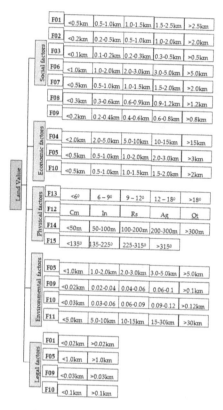

Here we can see that the economic benefit of being on the coast is most strongly felt if you're within half a kilometer of the ocean, but the environmental effect (e.g., risk of flooding) is most strongly felt when you're within 0.03 kilometers. And so on and so forth. Your experts help you work out all these rules. Note that for a few of these factors (such as land use and slope), you use metrics other than distance (e.g. land use classification and grade).

Then you take all that stuff and assign everything a value between 0 and 5.

Table 1. Scores of land valuation sub-factors.

	Code	Name	Unit	5	4	3	2	1	0
Social	F01	National Road	km	<0.5	0.5-1.0	1.0-1.5	1.5-2.5	2.5-3.0	>3.0
	F02	Mun/City Road	km	<0.2	0.2-0.5	0.5-1.0	1.0-2.0	2.0-2.5	>2.5
	F03	Barangay Road	km	<0.01	0.1-0.2	0.2-0.3	0.3-0.5	0.5-1.0	>1.0
	F06	Hospitals	km	<1.0	1.0-2.0	2.0-3.0	3.0-5.0	5.0-5.5	>5.5
	F07	University	km	<0.5	0.5-1.0	1.0-1.5	1.5-2.0	2.0-2.5	>2.5
	F08	Secondary Sch.	km	<0.3	0.3-0.6	0.6-0.9	0.9-1.2	1.2-1.5	>1.5
	F09	Freshwater	km	<0.2	0.2-0.4	0.4-0.6	0.6-0.8	0.8-1.0	>1.0
Economic	F04	CBD	km	<2.0	2.0-5.0	5-10.0	10-15.0	15-20.0	>20.0
	F05	Industry	km	<0.5	0.5-1.0	1.0-2.0	2.0-3.0	3.0-3.5	>3.5
	F10	Coastline	km	<0.5	0.5-1.0	1.0-1.5	1.5-2.0	2.0-2.5	>2.5
Physical	F12	Landuse	-	Cm	In	Rs	Ag	Ot	-
	F13	Slope	°	<6	6-9	9-12	12-18	>18	-
	F14	Elevation	m	<50	50-100	100-200	200-300	300-500	-
	F15	Aspect	°	<135	-	135-225	225-315	>315	-
Environmental	F05	Industry	km	>5.0	3.0-5.0	2.0-3.0	1.0-2.0	<1.0	-
	F09	Freshwater	km	>0.1	0.06-0.1	0.04-0.06	0.02-0.04	<0.02	-
	F10	Coastline	km	>0.12	0.09-0.12	0.06-0.09	0.03-0.06	<0.03	-
	F11	Faultzone[1]	km	>30	15-30.0	10-15.0	5.0-10	<5.0	-
Legal	F01	National Road	km	>0.02	-	-	-	<0.02	-
	F05	Industry	km	>1.0	-	-	-	<1.0	-
	F09	Freshwater	km	>0.03	-	-	-	<0.03	-
	F10	Coastline	km	>0.1	-	-	-	<0.1	-

[1] 100-m (both side) from active Faultline, based on [29] study.

Your team of experts then uses this table to come up with a set of weights for everything.

Table 3. Pair-wise comparison and weights of main factors.

	Physical	Social	Economic	Environment	Legal	Weights
Physical	1	1/3	1/2	2	4	0.184
Social	3	1	3	3	5	0.432
Economic	2	1/3	1	2	2	0.201
Environment	1/2	1/3	1/2	1	1	0.101
Legal	1/4	1/5	1/2	1	1	0.082

CR = 0.06

Table 4. Pair-wise comparison and weights of sub-factors.

a. Physical factors						b. Legal factors				
	F13	F14	F15	F12	Weights		F01	F05	F09	F10 Weights
F13	1	2	3	1/3	0.237	F01	1	1	3	1/2 0.265
F14	1/2	1	2	1/3	0.151	F05	1	1	2	1 0.275
F15	1/3	1/2	1	1/6	0.080	F09	1/3	1/2	1	1/2 0.128
F12	3	3	6	1	0.532	F10	2	1	2	1 0.332

CR = 0.02 (Physical)   CR = 0.05 (Legal)

c. Social factors								
	F01	F02	F03	F06	F07	F08	F09	Weights
F01	1	2	3	1	2	1	5	0.223
F02	1/2	1	1	1/2	1/3	1	4	0.113
F03	1/3	1	1	1	2	1	4	0.145
F06	1	2	1	1	3	2	5	0.220
F07	1/2	3	1/2	1/3	1	1/2	3	0.119
F08	1	1	1	1/2	2	1	2	0.139
F09	1/5	1/4	1/4	1/5	1/3	1/2	1	0.041

CR = 0.07

d. Economic factors					e. Environmental factors				
	F04	F05	F10	Weights		F05	F09	F11	F10 Weights
F04	1	3	2	0.539	F05	1	1	1/2	1 0.204
F05	1/3	1	1/2	0.164	F09	1	1	1/2	1 0.204
F10	1/2	2	1	0.297	F11	2	2	1	1 0.346
					F10	1	1	1	1 0.246

CR = 0.01 (Economic)   CR = 0.02 (Environmental)

What essentially comes out of this is a big linear equation with a bunch of coefficients for every one of your factors, which is then broadly fit to the observed market prices. When you're done, you can take any property on your list, multiply each of its characteristics by its respective weight, run that through your equation, and calculate the predicted price of the land.

How accurate is it? The authors compare it to standard Multiple Regression Analysis and claim it fares better.

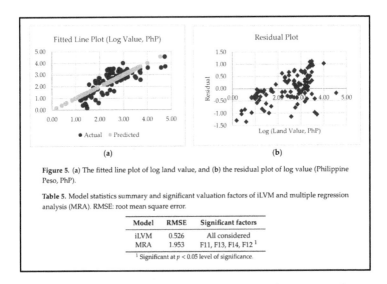

Figure 5. (a) The fitted line plot of log land value, and (b) the residual plot of log value (Philippine Peso, PhP).

Table 5. Model statistics summary and significant valuation factors of iLVM and multiple regression analysis (MRA). RMSE: root mean square error.

Model	RMSE	Significant factors
iLVM	0.526	All considered
MRA	1.953	F11, F13, F14, F12 [1]

[1] Significant at $p < 0.05$ level of significance.

Root Mean Square Error (the key test metric) is quite a bit less than MRA. In addition, I *think* it is also saying that the MRA algorithm decided that only four of the factors were significant and basically ignored all the rest. By contrast, iLVM was able to maintain contributions from all the factors, because it doesn't leave that decision to the computer. The wording in the paper isn't entirely clear, so the above is my best guess at what it seems to be saying.

The authors claim that about 67% of the variability is explained by their model, but they note that there are some areas where the model can be off by more than a factor of 1.0 in either the positive or negative direction.

One thing that's kind of fun about this model is that you can make neat graphs like this that show the individual contribution of each factor:

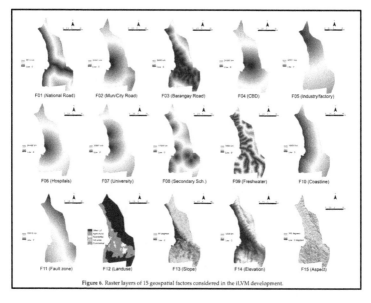

Figure 6. Raster layers of 15 geospatial factors considered in the iLVM development.

The main downside to this model is that it relies on a whole lot of subjective expert opinion and can be questioned on that basis. That said, it can be cheaply deployed in a transparent and consistent way across a large area. You can see why that's attractive for a developing nation with weak institutions and poor market transaction records; the argument is that this is a significant improvement over the former status quo.

I wonder how well this model performs when you feed it better market transaction data, and how that would compare against all the others methods under identical conditions. More research is needed.

Rather than drag you through several dozen more research papers that I consulted in my own research, why don't I just leave a list of some of the most interesting ones here, for those interested in pursuing these questions further:

- "Fuzzy Expert System for Land Valuation in Land Consolidation Processes" (Kilić, Rogulj, & Jajac, 2019)

- "Asset Appraisal Method Based on the Analytic Network Process" (Aragonés-Beltrán, García-Melón, Aznar, & Guijarro, 2009)

- "Land Valuation Using C5.0 with a Boosting Decision Tree" (Xue, Hu, Yang, & Chen, 2008)

- "PariTOP: A Goal Programming-Based Software for Real Estate Assessment" (Kettani & Khelifi, 2001)

- "Property Taxation and Mass Appraisal Valuations in Australia—Adapting to a New Environment" (Hefferan & Boyd, 2010)

- "Valuation and Assessment of Immovable Property" (Almy, 2014)

Nor should I fail to mention *Fundamentals of Mass Appraisal*, a literal textbook published by the IAAO, written by Gloudemans and Almy in 2011.

I've only scratched the surface here. There are a whole lot more methodology papers out there, and this is just a sample of the ones I happened to come across. They seem to fall into either "hands-off" or "hands-on" approaches, depending on how much direct human judgment you want to bake into the system.

So, can we accurately assess land and improvements separately?

Given the literature, and the state of the research, I think the answer is yes—it is quite plausible to believe that we can do so. That does not mean that there are no problems or difficulties left to navigate, but certainly, if the objection can be stated as "valuing land separately from improvements is fundamentally impossible, and we can never get better at it, so we shouldn't try," I think that's plainly ruled out.

We clearly have a variety of methods at our disposal that seem reasonably accurate. Each of them has particular strengths and weaknesses, and each directly addresses shortcomings of prior methods. All of this implies that this is something we can continue to improve at. The big questions are whether we've already arrived at "good enough" and how tight our error tolerances need to be.

The operative phrase very much is "good enough." I don't know of anywhere in the world that currently has a 100% LVT policy, let alone an 85% LVT. The lower your LVT, the greater your margin of error becomes for not taxing more than the true land value. I know plenty of Georgists who would be ecstatic if they could get a 75% LVT, or even a 50% LVT, implemented in their area.

Now, just because these assessment methods are available doesn't mean they're actually being used. Not everyone has Ted Gwartney as their assessor. Plenty of counties in my local area exclusively use the cost approach and will even apply a blanket "neighborhood factor" multiplier to up-assess swiftly appreciating areas. However, they apply that multiplier to the *buildings* rather than the land, which feels exactly backwards. The assessor hasn't raised the value of my land in years, while the assessed value of my house (which I am eminently qualified to tell you is an ever-degrading money pit) somehow continues to go up.

Good assessment depends on having well-trained staff, up-to-date methodology, and access to high quality market transaction data. I'm convinced, based on these papers and the IAAO's surveys, that assessment doesn't require a huge army of assessors poring over every aspect of citizens' properties.

Furthermore, plenty of places already have property tax systems in place and are already paying the full cost of property assessments and property tax collection. Many of the methods described above seem capable of reducing property assessment costs by focusing on the land first and foremost and letting the building's value fall out as a residual, as Ted Gwartney insists the procedure should be.

The cost also seems like something that, done properly, is only going to come down over time as fewer assessors are required. Another option is to keep staff sizes the same but use the emerging productivity gains to increase the frequency and quality of assessments. It also seems clear to me that Land Value Taxation is not *more* invasive and expensive than income and sales tax when you factor in the cost of compliance (not to mention the deadweight loss imposed on the economy).

Countries that have implemented Land Value Taxes, such as Denmark, are already seeing some of the claims of Georgism borne out, as we discussed in Part III. This suggests to me that modern methods are probably "good enough," so long as assessors are well trained, abiding by current best practices, and able to access good market data.

This book was originally posted as a series of articles on Astral Codex Ten, a blog where ideas as lofty as full brain uploading, superhuman AI, and biological immortality are frequently discussed in earnest. Compared to all that, it doesn't seem outlandish to suggest that human beings can probably use math and science to get better at estimating the market value of land relative to buildings.

CONCLUSION
By George, Unimproved Land Value can (probably) be accurately assessed.

Part V

Conclusions & Next Steps

26

Moving Forward

By George, the evidence has convinced me of three things:

☑ Land is a really big deal

☑ Land Value Tax cannot be passed on to tenants

☑ Land Value can (probably) be accurately assessed

I humbly submit that the case for Georgism survives a summary dismissal and can move on to a trial of the particulars.

Where do we go from here?

In the course of writing this series, I found a few subjects that someone should just go ahead and test already.

These subjects are:

1. ASSESSMENT METHODS

A lot of the methodology papers I read only test one or two methods at a time in a particular case study. What I couldn't find was a study that tests *every* major mass appraisal method in one big cross comparison study, all in the same physical location using the same dataset. If we had this, we could get a better sense of their strengths and weaknesses without wondering what differences are due simply to one study being in Germany and the other in the Philippines.

It seems the necessary ingredients are:

- An ideal test location with excellent property records and (ideally) a history of quality land value assessment and/or Land Value Tax

- Experienced local assessment experts with knowledge of the area

- Data scientists, statisticians, and machine learning nerds

I'm told by some friends who know this kind of stuff that the ideal location in the United States would likely be somewhere in Pennsylvania, a state with LVT friendly policies and a history of detailed property records.

After that, you'd pick out every mass assessment methodology from the literature, line them up, and reproduce them. Then, you'd come up with a novel method or two of your own and test those, too. Finally, you'd come up with a validation strategy for testing against true market selling values. The chief goals here would be to:

- Evaluate the current state of the art. How wide are the error bars?

- See if you can improve on the state of the art. How close to ground truth can you get?

Once the first study is done, you'd want to test it in another area—maybe Australia, Denmark, Germany, or the Philippines. If Georgism is true, and the only thing standing in the way is being able to pull off accurate assessments, then let's just get better at doing that. We're the species that split the atom and travelled to the moon. Surely, we can handle this.

2. TOTAL LAND VALUE OF THE UNITED STATES

It's really annoying that we don't confidently know this figure, and it has huge implications for LVT policy. Technically, this is an "assessment" problem, but in practice, when you're assessing *the entire USA,* you're often falling back on big black-box buckets of aggregated property values rather than building a database of direct ground-truth market transactions yourself.

In Part II, we saw how big the difference was between Albouy, who used pure land sales directly from the market, and Larson, who applied the cost approach to official figures. If one of you readers has MLS access for all 50 states and/or a bunch of other records, it'd be interesting to see if we could settle this debate once and for all.

3. A PUSH FOR MORE OPEN REAL ESTATE MARKET TRANSACTION DATA

To my knowledge, there's no good, one-stop shop for solid, historical, ground truth real estate market transaction data that's uniform and detailed across the entire United States. I'm well aware of how important access to solid data is for researchers. I run a site called gamedatacrunch.com that just quietly scrapes public metrics from the PC video game store Steam (they don't mind—I asked). I'm constantly getting requests from researchers to dump slices from my DB for them, which I'm always happy to do. If not for making this data available, those research papers might not be happening.

So many questions that are answerable in principle go unanswered in practice simply for want of access to data. Smart people then make bad policy decisions out of ignorance.

In principle, I suppose someone could set up a script that scrapes listing prices from Zillow and Redfin all day, every day, but I'm not sure what the long-term legal status of such an operation would be.

If you're a billionaire who wants to do something for Georgism, instead of building a $400 billion super city in the desert[13], you could buy the real estate listing service Redfin for less than 1% of that (CompaniesMarketCap.com, 2022) and make their data available to researchers.

In any case, whether improved access to consistent, country-wide data were to come from data mining or repeal of real estate non-disclosure laws, it would be an invaluable resource for researchers.

4. EMPIRICAL EXAMINATION OF ATCOR

If ATCOR (All Taxes Come Out of Rent) holds up empirically, it would be a huge deal. Then, it wouldn't matter whose land value estimates you accept, because you'd always be able to shift taxes off of income and capital and onto land without losing revenue. Mason Gaffney cites a few cases where it is supposed to have been observed in his 2009 piece,

---

[13]Billionaire Marc Lore has proposed building a planned city called "Telosa" with a Land Value Tax governance model

"The Hidden Taxable Capacity of Land," but we could really dig into this further (Gaffney, 2009). A claim this tantalizing really needs to be nailed down and resolved once and for all.

5. RESPONSES TO COMMENTS

I've been absolutely drowning in feedback since this book was first posted as a series of articles, and there's no way I'll be able to address everything here. Doing full justice to some of these will require future articles and revisions of this book, but I can leave some brief notes here.

ZONING

Many people replied that Land Value Tax is useless until or unless you fix zoning. First of all, Georgists are natural allies in fixing restrictive zoning policies. This is something they definitely want and will fight for. Second, one of the reasons for restrictive zoning policies is broken incentives. A city doesn't have a huge incentive to repeal restrictive zoning policies because it isn't hurting their tax base. According to Georgists, a city whose tax base is its land value has well-aligned incentives. It is incentivized to maximize land value by making the city a more desirable place to live, which also raises its tax base. It is dis-incentivized to over-assess or over-tax the land, however, because that will cause people to leave, which will lower their land values and also their tax base. One of the principal things that depresses land values and the tax base in this scenario is restrictive zoning. I personally don't care whether you first pass LVT or first repeal restrictive zoning, you can and should do both. Either one helps the other along.

CORRUPTION

Some people agreed to all of the points raised *in theory*, but pointed out that human beings are wicked sinners, and LVT will be bent towards the malevolent will of our overlords, just like the old policies. They're not wrong!

The problem with this argument is that it is a fully general argument against change. The overlords game *every* system to their benefit. Rely on standardized tests? They'll game the SAT's with phony disability accommodations and outright cheating. Abolish standardized tests? They'll make their kids take fifty extracurriculars and pay a ghost writer to pen their college entrance essay about their life-changing volunteer work in Ghana.

The right question is not "can the rich game this system?" but rather, "can they game it *less* than the existing one?" This is why we should keep standardized tests, even though rich people can and do game them. (The evidence shows that, on balance, standardized tests are one of the few ways a minority student from a poor background even has a chance to move upwards (Bhavnani, 2020) (Harris, 2020).)

The chief way you can game Land Value Tax is to cozy up to your local assessor and get them to say your valuable land is actually garbage and it shouldn't be taxed much. I grant that motivated people could plausibly pull this off to various degrees, but you have to do this kind of corruption in the open. Your land value assessment is public record, highly visible on a map, and will stick out like a sore thumb.

You might be able to get the assessor to lie about your *land value*, but what's the status quo we're comparing against? We don't even *know* how much *cash money value* is being socked away in Switzerland and the Caymans, let alone by whom. Even if we did, good luck figuring out how to lure that back to a taxable jurisdiction. Land can't run or hide. Best of all, you can't evade Land Value Taxes by obscuring land ownership through shell corporations, because the tax doesn't care who owns it.

My dream is for us to commoditize open-source mass appraisal systems and push for public real estate transaction records everywhere, so that organizations and educated members of the public can do their own land value audits at scale.

Again, this is something that just needs to be subjected to empirics. We can sling theory back and forth at each other all day, but the proof is in the pudding. There are places that have done Land Value Tax in the past, and there are places that do it today. A good candidate for future study is looking at case studies of where LVT has been tried and explicitly look for this problem.

Finally, defeatism is corruption's best friend. *If* you believe everything I'm saying here, *and* your only obstacle is fear of corruption, *and* you accept that LVT's vulnerability to corruption is not any worse than the status quo's...then why not just get out there and fight for the world you want to see? Nothing good ever came without a struggle.

6. Future Direction

This is only the first edition of this book, and it won't be the last. I will continue to post future chapters to my websites LANDISABIGDEAL.COM and GAMEOFRENT.COM, which will eventually make their way into future revisions (or volumes) of this book.

First, I will add a few in-depth case studies where Georgist Land Value Tax policies have been partially implemented in the past (England, 2015).

Second, I will add a section concerning the management of natural resources, a special kind of Economic Land. I will put a particular focus on Norway, whose resource management system is arguably quite Georgist (Brigham & Moses, 2021).

Third, I will add a section discussing "virtual real estate" in multiplayer online games, virtual worlds, and the so-called "metaverse." I will discuss how game developers have been consistently re-creating the problems of land speculation in their digital worlds for decades (Doucet & Cook, 2022).

Finally, I plan to expand and update the section on real estate assessment. With the help of some grant money from Astral Codex Ten, I have put together a team that is actively working on applying state of the art research to several American cities. Future revisions will include the results of our research.

By George, let's make the same kinds of step-by-step improvements to our neighborhoods, cities, countries, and eventually, the entire world.

Acknowledgements

I would like to thank the following people and organizations without whom this book would not have been possible:

- My wonderful wife Emily, for everything

- Scott Alexander for running the Book Review contest, and the ACX community for selecting me as the winner

- Count Bla for going above and beyond the call of duty with suggestions, research help, and general support

- Alexandra Elbakyan for lifting the boot of deadweight loss off the necks of researchers worldwide

- James Cavin and Fr. Cassian Sibley for help with editing and proofreading

- Ted Gwartney for his seminar, and for putting up with all of my annoying questions

- Nicolaus Tideman for providing feedback and sources

- Slime Mold Time Mold for help with structure, scope, and editing

- Will Jarvis for helpful comments, discussions, and sources

- Nate Blair and BlueRepublik for feedback, charts, and editing tips on both the original book review and this piece

- Matthew Yglesias for his land value estimation method

- Noah Smith for helpful comments and advice from an economist's perspective

- Jerusalem Desmas for her research and insights

- Erusian for giving a helpful and detailed account of objections to Georgism

- The Georgist twitter DM group for drowning me in articles, citations, and sources

- Common Ground USA, Prosper Australia, The Henry George School of Social Science, The Center for Property Tax Reform, and The Robert Schalkenbach Foundation for their research, insights, educational efforts, and organizing

- Dan Sullivan, Mark Mollineaux, and Wyn Achenbaum for useful comments, sources, and help.

- Pyradius for pointing me towards *Counting Bounty*

- Bill Newell, for the memes

- /r/georgism for helpful sources and articles

- The authors of all the cited research papers

- The "old guard" of the 20th century Georgist movement for maintaining historical documents and research papers into the present day

- Henry George, for planting trees in whose shade he would never sit

Glossary

ATCOR: "All Taxes Come Out of Rent," a theory most commonly associated with Mason Gaffney, which proposes that, all else being equal, any reductions in taxes will result in a proportional increase in land rental values.

AUSTERITY: An economic policy position that seeks to keep the budget balanced principally through cutting spending and/or raising taxes.

CAPITAL: Wealth set to the purpose of gaining more wealth.

DEADWEIGHT LOSS: The amount of economic activity lost to society when supply and demand can not reach their natural equilibrium because of an external constraint, such as a tax.

ECONOMIC RENT: The amount of money a factor of production receives as its return that exceeds the minimum amount necessary to bring it into production.

FACTORS OF PRODUCTION: Any one of the three things which are involved in producing wealth: Land, Labor, and Capital.

GEOGRAPHIC INFORMATION SYSTEMS (GIS): Any technological system that allows for the processing and/or visualization of data in the form of maps.

GROSS DOMESTIC INCOME (GDI): The total income a country collectively earns from all the goods and services it produces in a particular amount of time. In theory, Gross Domestic Income and Gross Domestic Product should be equal, but they are measured in different ways and based on different data sources, so there can be discrepancies.

GROSS DOMESTIC PRODUCT (GDP): The total market value of all goods and services a country collectively produces in a particular amount of time. One of the most important high-level statistics for comparing countries by economic productivity.

GROUND RENT: The recurring rental value of a piece of land, excluding the value of all improvements.

IMPROVEMENTS: In the context of real estate, anything that adds value to a land parcel other than the land itself. Typically, this means buildings, but could also include organic and agricultural contributions such as soil improvements, crops, irrigation, orchards, etc.

INTEREST: George's term for the return to capital.

LABOR: The exertion of human beings.

LABOR THEORY OF VALUE: An economic theory associated with Karl Marx, which says that a thing's value is tied to the amount of "socially necessary labor" required to produce it.

LAND: All natural materials, forces, and opportunities. This includes the conventional definition of physical land,

but also natural resources, locations, and things like
electromagnetic spectrum, orbital real estate, etc.

LAND REFORM: Any policy under which land ownership is
changed. Typically this is shorthand for Land
redistribution, where large estates are broken up into
smaller parcels and given out to new, formerly
landless, owners.

LAND RENTAL VALUE: The recurring rental income that a
plot of land can fetch in the market. Alternatively,
the monetary price of the recurring benefits that
accrue to the owner for holding the land.

LAND SELLING VALUE: The price to purchase a plot land.

LAND VALUE: An ambiguous term that refers to the price
land fetches in the market, but doesn't indicate
whether it means rental or selling value. In the
context of "Land Value Tax," it means rental value.

LAND VALUE TAX (LVT): A recurring tax on the rental value
of land. A "100% LVT" would be a recurring charge
equal not to the selling price of the land, but to the
recurring income the land can generate.

MALTHUSIANISM: A philosophy ascribed to English cleric
Thomas Malthus, which ascribes economic crises to
the exponential growth of the human population,
which must necessarily end in catastrophe. It has
been widely discredited in the modern day.

MARGIN OF PRODUCTION: The most productive land
available that can be had without paying rent.

MARGINAL THEORY OF VALUE: The economic theory of value held by most non-Marxist/Marxian economists, including Henry George. This states that the value of a thing is whatever the market is willing to pay to acquire it.

MONOPOLY: From the Greek for "one seller," any economic sector where production is dominated by one agent.

MULTIPLE REGRESSION ANALYSIS: A statistical method used to deduce/estimate the relationship between a set of variables.

NATIONAL CAPITAL: A measure of a country's wealth, which sums up all forms of capital. This uses a conventional definition of "capital" which includes many things that George would exclude: namely land, natural resources, and financial instruments.

NIMBY: "Not In My Back Yard," an epithet for people who organize to oppose new construction in their local areas, especially those opposed to new housing. The natural opponents of YIMBYs.

PRODUCE: Wealth produced by production. AKA: product.

PRODUCTION: Labor applied to the production of wealth.

REAL ASSETS: Private property in anything tangible, such as land, buildings, natural resources, machines, tools, etc. This specifically excludes financial assets and money.

REAL ESTATE: Private property in land, buildings, or both.

RENT: George's term for the return to land.

SINGLE TAX: A maximalist Georgist position under which Land Value Tax is the only tax.

TAMMANY HALL: A powerful and corrupt political machine that dominated New York politics in the 19th century.

TARIFF: A tax levied on imported goods, often as a measure to protect local industries by artificially increasing the price of foreign goods.

UNIVERSAL BASIC INCOME (UBI): A social policy by which every citizen of a polity receives a guaranteed recurring minimum income payment regardless of employment status. An outgrowth of an earlier concept known as the "Citizen's Dividend."

WAGES: George's term for the return to labor.

WEALTH: That which is produced when nature's bounty is touched by human labor resulting in a tangible product that is the object of human desire.

YIMBY: "Yes In My Back Yard," an epithet for those who support new construction in their local areas; the natural opponents of NIMBYs. YIMBYs typically lobby for zoning reform, repeal of mandatory parking minimums, and other exclusionary and wasteful land use policies.

Bibliography

Airi, N., Dadayan, L., & Rueben, K. (2021). *State and Local Finance Data: Exploring the Census of Governments*. Retrieved from Tax Policy Center: https://state-local-finance-data.taxpolicycenter.org/pages.cfm

Al. (2011, June 11). *100-Year Housing Price Index History*. Retrieved from Observations: https://web.archive.or g/web/20210208185441/https:/observationsandnote s.blogspot.com/2011/06/us-housing-prices-since-1900.html

Albouy, D., Ehrlich, G., & Shin, M. (2017, June). Metropolitan Land Values. *The Review of Economics and Statistics*, 454-466. doi:http://doi.org/10.1162/rest_a_00710

Albouy, D., Ehrlich, G., & Shin, M. (2017). *Online Appendix to "Metropolitan Land Values."* The Review of Economics and Statistics. Retrieved from MIT Press: https://direct.mit.edu/rest/article-abstract/100/3/454/58476/Metropolitan-Land-Values?redirectedFrom=fulltext

Alexander, S. (2014, December 12). *Beware the Man of One Study*. Retrieved from Slate Star Codex: https://slatestarcodex.com/2014/12/12/beware-the-man-of-one-study/

Alexander, S. (2017, February 9). *Considerations on Cost Disease*. Retrieved from SlateStarCodex: https://slatestarcodex.com/2017/02/09/considerations-on-cost-disease/

Almy, R. (2014). Valuation and Assessment of Immovable Property. *OECD Working Papers on Fiscal Federalism, 19*. doi:10.1787/5jz5pzvr28hk-en.

Almy, R., & Gloudemans, R. (2011). *Fundamentals of Mass Appraisal*. Kansas City, Missouri: International Association of Assessment Officers.

American Enterprise Institute. (2021, May). *Land Price and Land Share Indicators*. Retrieved from American Enterprise Institute: https://www.aei.org/housing/land-price-indicators/

Amoros, R. (2019, January 28). *Price Changes Over the Last 20 Years Prove the Economy is Rigged*. Retrieved from howmuch.net: https://web.archive.org/web/20210301102455/https://howmuch.net/articles/price-changes-in-usa-in-past-20-years

Andelson, R. V. (2003, January 7). On Separating the Landowner's Earned and Unearned Increment: A Georgist Rejoinder to F. A. Hayek. *The American Journal of Economics and Sociology, 59*(1), 109-117. doi:10.1111/1536-7150.00016

Appelbaum, B. (2021, July 19). *Good Riddance, TurboTax. Americans Need a Real 'Free File' Program*. Retrieved from The New York Times: https://www.

nytimes.com/2021/07/19/opinion/intuit-turbotax-free-filing.html

Aragonés-Beltrán , P., García-Melón, M., Aznar, J., & Guijarro, F. (2009). Asset Appraisal Method Based on the Analytic Network Process. *XIII Congreso Internacional de Ingeniería de Proyectos*, 726-737. Badajoz.

Arbor. (2021). *Q1 2021 Single-Family Rental Investment Trends Report*. Retrieved from Arbor: https://arbor.com/research/q1-2021-single-family-rental-investment-trends-report/#leadbot-0e2c1a70-f989dce9-fb3c0420-b714ffff4

Associated Press. (2014, November 17). *Number Of Homeless Children In U.S. At All-Time High; California Among Worst States*. Retrieved from CBS SF Bay Area: https://web.archive.org/web/201 60324104539/https:/sanfrancisco.cbslocal.com/2014 /11/17/number-of-homeless-children-in-u-s-at-all-time-high-california-among-worst-states/

Barr, J., Smith, F. H., & Kulkarni, S. J. (2018, May). What's Manhattan worth? A land values index from 1950 to 2014. *Regional Science and Urban Economics, 70*, 1-19. doi:https://doi.org/10.1016/j.regsciurbeco.2018.02.0 03

Barron, I. (1988, September/October). What Price USA inc? *Land & Liberty?*, 80. Retrieved from Cooperative Individualism: https://cooperative-individualism.org/barron-ian_steven-cord-challenges-economists-on-the-lack-of-land-value-data-1988-sep-oct.pdf

Bencure, J., Tripathi, N., Miyazaki, H., Ninsawat, S., & Kim, S. (2019, 7). Development of an Innovative Land Valuation Model (iLVM) for Mass Appraisal Application in Sub-Urban Areas Using AHP: An Integration of Theoretical and Practical Approaches. *Sustainability.* doi: http://dx.doi.org/10.3390/su11133731

Bhavnani, K.-K. (2020, February 3). RE: Systemwide Review of the Report of the Academic Council's Standardized Testing Task Force (STTF). Oakland, California, USA. Retrieved from UCLA: https://dms.senate.ucla.edu/issues/issue/?2548.Systemwide.Senate.Review.Report.of.the.Standardized.Testing.Task.Force

Bikas, K. (2018, June). *How Has Bank Lending Fared Since the Crisis?* Retrieved from PositiveMoney: https://positivemoney.org/2018/06/how-has-bank-lending-fared-since-the-crisis/

Blanco, M. A., Bauluz, L. E., & Martínez-Toledano, C. (2018). *Wealth in Spain, 1900-2014: A Country of Two Lands.* Paris, France: World Wealth & Income Database. doi: https://doi.org/10.1093/ej/ueaa103

BlueRepublik. (2019, July 31). *Welfare Economics and the Land Value Tax.* Retrieved from The Back Channel: https://web.archive.org/web/20210418033418/https

://bluerepublik.wordpress.com/2019/07/31/welfare-
economics-of-the-land-value-tax/

BlueRepublik. (2020, April 28). *No, Georgism is Still Sane.*
Retrieved from The Back Channel: https://web.arch
ive.org/web/20210703131232/https://bluerepublik.w
ordpress.com/2020/04/28/no-georgism-is-still-sane/

Borge, L.-E., & Rattsø, J. (2014). Capitalization of Property
Taxes in Norway. *Public Finance Review, 42* (5),
635-661. doi:10.1177/1091142113489845

Bosch, D., & Gray, G. (2018, April 16). *Tax Day 2018:
Compliance Costs Approach $200 Billion.* Retrieved
from American Action Forum: https://www.america
nactionforum.org/research/tax-day-2018-compliance-
costs-approach-200-billion/

Bourassa, S. C. (1987, October). Land Value Taxation and
New Housing Development in Pittsburgh. *Growth
and Change: a Journal of Urban and Regional Policy,
18*(4), 44-56. doi:10.1111/j.1468-2257.1987.tb
00087.x

Breckenfeld, G. (1983, August 8). Higher Taxes that
Promote Development. *Fortune*, 68-71.

Britannica, E. (2013, July 1). *Rent.* Retrieved from
Encyclopaedia Britannica: https://www.britannica.
com/topic/rent-economics

Brookhiser, R. (1993, October 1). *1886: The Men Who
Would be Mayor.* Retrieved from City Journal:
https://web.archive.org/web/20200926024934/htt

ps://www.city-journal.org/html/1886-men-who-would-be-mayor-12622.html

Buckley, W. F. (2000, April 2). In Depth with William F. Buckley Jr. (Interview on Book TV, CSPAN). (A. Caller, Interviewer) Retrieved from Youtube: https://www.youtube.com/watch?v=SRnTesZNH_g

Buettner, T. (2003). *Tiebout Visits Germany: Land Tax Capitalization in a Sample of German Municipalities.* Munich, Germany: Third Norwegian-German Seminar on Public Economics.

Capozza, D. R., Green, R. K., & Hendershott, P. H. (1996). Taxes, Mortgage Borrowing, and Residential Land Prices. In *Economic effects of fundamental tax reform* 171-210. Brookings Institution Press.

Coldwell Banker Richard Ellis. (2019). *North America Cap Rate Survey H1 2019.* Retrieved from CBRE: https://www.cbre.us/research-and-reports/North-America-Cap-Rate-Survey-H1-2019

Coldwell Banker Richard Ellis. (2020). *Cap Rate Survey Special Report Q3 2020.* Retrieved from CBRE: https://web.archive.org/web/ 20210806054719/ http:/cbre.vo.llnwd.net/grgservices/secure/US%20Cap%20Rate%20Survey%20Q3%202020.pdf?e=16282 28873&h=a614ce876e66ea42c9785fbba27a658c

Chesterton, G. K. (1920). *The Superstition of Divorce.* New York: John Lane.

Choi, K. W., & Sjoquist, D. L. (2015, August). Economic and Spatial Effects of Land Value Taxation in an Urban Area: An Urban Computable General Equilibrium Approach. *Land Economics, 91*(3), 536-555. Retrieved from https://www.researchgate.net/publication/228366356_Evidence_on_the_Distributional_Effects_of_a_Land_Value_Tax_on_Residential_Households

CompaniesMarketCap.com. (2022, February). *Market Capitalization of Redfin (RDFN)*. Retrieved from CompaniesMarketCap.com: https://web.archive.org/web/20211205031044/https:/companiesmarketcap.com/redfin/marketcap/

Congressional Budget Office. (2020, April 15). *The Federal Budget in 2019: An Infographic*. Retrieved from Congressional Budget Office: https://www.cbo.gov/publication/56324

Credit Suisse. (2020). *Global Wealth Report 2020*. Zürich, Switzerland: Credit Suisse. Retrieved from https://www.credit-suisse.com/media/assets/corporate/docs/about-us/research/publications/global-wealth-report-2020-en.pdf

Dahl, G., Kreiner, C., Nielsen, T., & Serena, B. (2020). *Linking Changes in Inequality in Life Expectancy and Mortality: Evidence from Denmark and the United States*. National Bureau of Economic Research. doi: https://doi.org/10.3386/w27509

Daley, B. (2020, July 2). *The Wild Decade: How the 1990s Laid the Foundations for Vladimir Putin's Russia*. Retrieved from The Conversation: https://theconvers ation.com/the-wild-decade-how-the-1990s-laid-the-foundations-for-vladimir-putins-russia-141098

Demographia. (2021, February 17). *New York Urbanized Area: Population & Density from 1800 (Provisional)*. Retrieved from Demographia: https://web.archive. org/web/20210217140046/http:/demographia.com/ db-nyuza1800.htm

Dorney, J. (2016, October 18). *The Greath Irish Famine 1845-1851 - A Brief Overview*. Retrieved from The Irish Story: https://web.archive.org/web/20220203 012651/https://www.theirishstory.com/2016/10/18/t he-great-irish-famine-1845-1851-a-brief-overview/

Dshort. (2010, September 21). *The Market and Recessions*. Retrieved from dshort.com: https://web.archive.org/ web/20100926130252/http://dshort.com/articles/re cessions.html

Dwyer, T. (2003). *The Taxable Capacity of Australian Land and Resources*. Sydney, Australia: Australian Tax Forum. Retrieved from Prosper Australia: https:// www.prosper.org.au/ wp-content/uploads/2007/11/ dwyer-tax-resources.pdf

Dyer, C. (2002). *Making a Living the Middle Ages: The People of Britain 850-1520*. New Haven, Connecticut: Yale University Press.

Ebeling, R. M. (2015, December 21). *There Is No Social Security Santa Claus*. Retrieved from The Future of Freedom Foundation: https://www.fff.org/explore-freedom/article/there-is-no-social-security-santa-claus/

Economist, The. (2019, October 19). *Homelessness is Declining in America, But it is Worsening in the Country's Most Prosperous Cities*. Retrieved from The Economist: https://web.archive.org/web/2021 0428222013/https://www.economist.com/united-states/2019/10/19/homelessness-is-declining-in-america

Economist, The. (2020, January 16). *How Housing Became the World's Biggest Asset Class*. Retrieved from The Economist: https://www.economist.com/special-report/2020/01/16/how-housing-became-the-worlds-biggest-asset-class

Economist, The. (2015, April 4). *The Paradox of Soil*. Retrieved from The Economist: https://www.economist.com/briefing/2015/04/04/the-paradox-of-soil

Edwards, M. E. (1984, October). Site Value Taxation on Australia. *The American Journal of Economics and Sociology, 43*(4), 481-495. doi:10.1111/j.1536-7150.1984.tb01876.x

Encyclopaedia Britannica. (2013, February 25). *Enclosure*. Retrieved from Encyclopaedia Britannica: https://www.britannica.com/topic/enclosure

Engels, F., & Marx, K. (1848). *Communist Manifesto.* Moscow: Progress Publishers.

Erb, K. P. (2016, January 20). *Report: Americans Spend More Than 8.9 Billion Hours Each Year On Tax Compliance.* Retrieved from Forbes: https://www. forbes.com/sites/kellyphillipserb/2016/06/20/report -americans-spend-more-than-8-9-billion-hours-each-year-on-tax-compliance/?sh=6d89670e3456

Evans, A. (2021, February 9). *Four Tricks for Fast Blurring in Software and Hardware.* Retrieved from Game Developer: https://www.gamedeveloper.com/ programming/four-tricks-for-fast-blurring-in-software-and-hardware

Explodicle (2008, March 17). Perfectly Inelastic Supply. Retrieved from Wikipedia: https://en.wikipedia.org/wiki/File: Perfectly_ inelastic_supply.svg license: CC BY-SA 3.0, https://creativecommons.org/licenses/by-sa/3.0/

Federal Reserve. (2000-2020). *Financial Accounts of the United States: Flow of Funds, Balance Sheets, and Integrated Macroeconomic Accounts.* Washington, D.C.: Federal Reserve. Retrieved from Federal Reserve: https://www.federalreserve.gov/releases/z1/

Finra. (2021). *Mortgage-Backed Securities.* Retrieved from Finra: https://www.finra.org/investors/learn-to-invest/types-investments/bonds/types-of-bonds/mortgage-backed-securities#:~:text=Mortgage

-backed%20securities,%20called%20MBS,million%20
worth%20of%20such%20mortgages.

Forsyth, T. (2021, January 11). *The History of the Landlord's
Game & Monopoly.* Retrieved from https://web.
archive.org/web/20210111131436/https://landlordsga
me.info/

Friedersdorf, C. (2018, June 4). *Op-Ed: After 40 years,
Proposition 13's failures are evident.* Retrieved from
Los Angeles Times: https://www.latimes.com/
opinion/op-ed/la-oe-friedersdorf-prop-13-20180604-
story.html

Friedman, M. (1978, February 6). "Is Tax Reform
Possible?". (E. Arten, Interviewer) Retrieved from
Youtube: https://youtu.be/8txLAkao6nI?t=3448

Fuest, C., Immel, L., Meier, V., & Neumeier, F. (2018,
August). Die Grundsteuer in Deutschland:
Finanzwissenschaftliche Analyse und
Reformoptionen. *ifo STUDIE.* Retrieved from ifo
Institut: https://www.ifo.de/publikationen/2018/
monographie-autorenschaft/die-grundsteuer-
deutschland-finanzwissenschaftliche

Gabriel, R. H. (1946). *The Course of American Democratic
Thought.* New York: Ronald Press Company.

Gaffney, M. (2005). *The Physiocratic Concept of ATCOR
(All Taxes Come Out of Rent).* Retrieved from
MasonGaffney.org: https://www.masongaffney.org/
workpapers/WP096%202005%20The%20Physiocrati
c%20Concept%20of%20ATCOR.pdf.

Gaffney, M. (2009). The Hidden Taxable Capacity of Land. *International Journal of Social Economics, 36*(4), 370-76. Retrieved from https://web.archive.org/web /20220122173833/https://thedepression.org.au/atco r/

Gallagher, J. (2020, July 15). *Fertility rate: 'Jaw-dropping' global crash in children being born.* Retrieved from BBC News: https://web.archive.org/web/20220204 030449/http://bbc.com/news/health-53409521

George, H. (1879). *Progress and Poverty.* San Francisco, California: W. M. Hinton and Company.

George, H. (1886). *Protection or Free Trade.* New York, New York: Doubleday, Page, and Company.

George, H. (1897). *The Science of Political Economy.* New York: Robert Schalkenbach Foundation.

Glasner, D. (1997). *Great Depression of 1873-1896.* New York: Garland Publishing.

Grosskopf, S. P., & Johnson, M. B. (1980). Land Value Tax Revenue Potentials: Methodology and Measurement. *Land Value Taxation: The Progress and Poverty Centenary*, 41-67.

Gwartney, T. (2021, August 23). 2010 Revaluation in Greenwich Connecticut: Henry George's Theories, Planning the Project and Applying Valuation Models. Henry George School of Social Science.

Gwartney, T. (2021, August 9). Assessment Policy &
    Administration Trends: Good Government and
    Statewide Differences in Property Tax Assessment
    Practices. Henry George School of Social Science.

Gwartney, T. (2021, August 2). Understanding Assessments:
    Introduction to Fundamentals of Assessment and the
    Role of the Assessor. Henry George School of Social
    Science.

Hacker News. (2021, February 14). "*Location-Based Pay*" -
    *Who Are We to Complain? (Hacker News
    comment thread).* Retrieved from Hacker News:
    https: //web.archive.org/web/20210907195847/
    https://news.ycombinator.com/item?id=26131138

Hagman, D. (1964-1965). The Single Tax and Land-Use
    Planning: Henry George Updated. *UCLA Law
    Review,* 762-788.

Hagman, D. G. (1978). "Land-Value Taxation." In D. G.
    Hagman, & D. J. Misczynski, *Windfalls For
    Wipeouts: Land Value Capture and Compensation.*
    Washington, D.C.: American Planning Association.
    Retrieved from Cooperative Individualism: https://
    www.cooperative-individualism.org/hagman-
    donald_land-value-taxation-1978.htm

Harris, C. (2020, Winter). The Right Measurement. *City
    Journal.* Retrieved from City Journal: https://www.
    city-journal.org/standardized-tests-student-merit

Hayek, F. A. (1960). *The Constitution of Liberty.* Chicago:
    University of Chicago Press, 1960.

Hayes, N. (2020). *The Book of Trespass: Crossing the Lines that Divide Us*. United Kingdom: Bloomsbury Publishing.

Hefferan, M. J., & Boyd, T. (2010). Property taxation and Mass Appraisal Valuations in Australia - Adapting to a New Environment. *Property Management, 28*(3), 149-162. doi:10.1108/02637471011051291

Hilber, C. A. (2017). The Economic Implications of House Price Capitalization: A Synthesis. *Real Estate Economics, 45*(2), 301-339.

Høj, A. K., Jørgensen, M. R., & Schou, P. (2017). *Land Taxes and Housing Prices*. Copenhagen, Denmark: De Økonomiske Råd. Retrieved from De Økonomiske Råd: https://dors.dk/files/media/publikationer/arbejdspapirer/2017/02_arbejdspapir_land_tax.pdf

Hudson, M. (2001, March 25). *Where Did All the Land Go?* Michael Hudson on Finance, Real Estate, and the Powers of Neoliberalism. Retrieved from Michael-Hudson.com: https://michael-hudson.com/2001/03/where-did-all-the-land-go-the-feds-new-balance-sheet-calculationsa-critique-of-land-value-statistics/

IAAO. (2013, April). *Standard On Ratio Studies: A criterion for measuring fairness, quality, equity and accuracy*. Retrieved from IAAO: https://www.iaao.org/media/standards/Standard_on_Ratio_Studies.pdf

IAAO. (2017). *PTAPP 2017 Data Summary.* Retrieved from IAAO: https://www.iaao.org/wcm/ Resources_Content/PTAPP.aspx

IAAO. (2020, January). *Standard on Property Tax Policy.* Retrieved from IAAO: https://www.iaao.org/media/ standards/Standard_on_Property_Tax_Policy.pdf

IRS. (2021, June 24). *IRS Budget & Workforce.* Retrieved from IRS: https://www.irs.gov/statistics/irs-budget-and-workforce

Jordà, Ò., Schularick, M., & Taylor, A. M. (2014). *The Great Mortgaging: Housing Finance, Crises, and Business Cycles.* Cambridge, MA: National Bureau of Economic Research.

Kapfidze, T. (2020, June 30). *LendingTree Reveals the Most Valuable Cities in America.* Retrieved from lendingtree: https://web.archive.org/web/20200716 152956/https:/www.lendingtree.com/home/mortgag e/lendingtree-reveals-the-most-valuable-cities-in-america/

Kettani, O., & Khelifi, K. (2001). PariTOP: A goal Programming-Based Software for Real Estate Assessment. *Eur. J. Oper. Res.*, 362-376.

Keynes, J. M. (1978). *The Collected Writings of John Maynard Keynes.* Royal Economic Society.

Kiel, P. (2019, May 30). *It's Getting Worse: The IRS Now Audits Poor Americans at About the Same Rate as the Top 1%.* Retrieved from PropUblica:

272

LAND IS A BIG DEAL

https://web.archive.org/web/20220216020610/https://www.propublica.org/article/irs-now-audits-poor-americans-at-about-the-same-rate-as-the-top-1-percent

Kilić, J., Rogulj, K., & Jajac, N. (2019). Fuzzy Expert System for Land Valuation in Land Consolidation Processes. *Croatian Operational Research Review, 10*(1). doi:10.17535/crorr.2019.0009

King, A. T. (1977). Estimating Property Tax Capitalization: A Critical Comment. *Journal of Political Economy, 85*(2), 425-431. doi:10.1086/260574

Kolbe, J., Schulz, R., Wersing, M., & Werwatz, A. (2015, February 25). Identifying Berlin's Land Value Map Using Adaptive Weights Smoothing. *Computational Statistics*, 767-790. doi:10.1007/s00180-015-0559-9

Kolbe, J., Schulz, R., Wersing, M., & Werwatz, A. (2019). Land Value Appraisal Using Statistical Methods. *Agricultural Land Markets - Efficiency and Regulation*. Retrieved from Humboldt-Universität zu Berlin: https://edoc.hu-berlin.de/bitstream/handle/18452/20511/FORLand-2019-07.pdf?sequence=1&isAllowed=y

Kulish, N., Livni, E., & Emma, G. (2021, November 2). *Who Are America's Billionaires, Anyway?* Retrieved from The New York Times: https://www.nytimes.com/2021/10/28/business/america-billionaires.html

Kuminoff, N. V., & Pope, J. C. (2013, February 1). The Value of Residential Land and Structures during the

Great Housing Boom and Bust. *Land Economics,* *89*(1), 1-29.

Land Equities. (2020, November 11). *38.1 Acres Off Grid Bordering BLM, Gerlach, Nevada.* Retrieved from Land Equities: https://web.archive.org/web/2020 1111232841/https://landequities.com/nevada/061-020-55

Larson, W. (2015). *New Estimates of Value of Land of the United States.* US Department of Commerce. Washington, DC: Bureau of Economic Analysis. Retrieved from https://web.archive.org/web/2022 0104231402/https://www.bea.gov/system/files/pape rs/WP2015-3.pdf

Larson, W. D., Davis, M. A., Oliner, S. D., & Shui, J. (2019/2020). *The Price of Residential Land for Counties, ZIP Codes, and Census Tracts in the United States.* Washington, DC: Federal Housing Finance Agency.

Lincoln Institute of Land Policy. (2017, November 21). *Land and Property Values in the U.S.* Retrieved from Lincoln Institute of Land Policy: https://web.archive. org/web/20171121002821/http:/datatoolkits.lincolnin st.edu/subcenters/land-values

Macrotrends. (2022). *Australia GNI 1964-2022.* Retrieved from macrotrends: https://www.macrotrends.net/ countries/AUS/australia/gni-gross-national-income

Macrotrends. (2022). *Australian - US Dollar Exchange Rate (AUD USD) - Historical Chart.* Retrieved from

macrotrends: https://www.macrotrends.net/2551/
australian-us-dollar-exchange-rate-historical-chart

Marx, K. (1975). *Karl Marx and Frederick Engels, Selected Correspondence.* Moscow: Progress Publishers.

Mills, D. E. (1981, March). The Non-Neutrality of Land Value Taxation. *National Tax Journal, 34*(1), 125-129. doi:10.1086/NTJ41862356

Moore, M. S. (2017, May 3). *This Land is Your Land.* Retrieved from Pacific Standard: https://web.archive.org/web/20220204070043/https://psmag.com/news/this-land-is-your-land-3392

Mott, F. L. (1947). *Golden Multitudes : The Story of Best Sellers in the United States.* New York, New York: Bowker.

Murphy, C. B. (2020, October 30). *Double Irish With a Dutch Sandwich.* Retrieved from Investopedia: https://web.archive.org/web/20220114015415/https://www.investopedia.com/terms/d/double-irish-with-a-dutch-sandwich.asp

NASBO. (2021). *State Expenditure Report.* Washington, DC: National Association of State Budget Officers.

New York Times, The. (1968, February 8). Major Describes Moves. *The New York Times*, 14.

Nock, A. J. (1933). Henry George: Unorthodox American. *Scribner's Magazine.* Retrieved from Wealth and

Want: http://wealthandwant.com/docs/
Nock_HGUA.htm

Oates, W. E. (1969, November/December). The Effects of Property Taxes and Local Public Spending on Property Values: An Empirical Study of Tax Capitalization and the Tiebout Hypothesis. *Journal of Political Economy, 77*(6), 957-971. Retrieved from JSTOR: https://www.jstor.org/stable/1837209

Palmon, O., & Smith, B. A. (1998). New Evidence on Property Tax Capitalization. *Journal of Political Economy, 106*(5), 1099-1111. doi:10.1086/250041

Pastoriza, J. J. (1915, March). The Houston Plan of Taxation. *The Annals of the American Academy of Political and Social Science*, 194-197. Retrieved from JSTOR: https://www.jstor.org/stable/1012861#metadata_info_tab_contents

Peters, G. (2021, May 28). *Federal Budget Receipts and Outlays*. Retrieved from The American Presidency Project: https://www.presidency.ucsb.edu/statistics/data/federal-budget-receipts-and-outlays

Piketty, T. (2014). *Capital in the Twenty-First Century*. Cambridge, Massachusetts: The Belknap Press of Harvard University Press.

Pillai, V. (1987, Occtober 1). Property Taxation in Thailand: An Uncommon Combination of a Land Tax and a Rental Tax. *Singapore Economic Review, 32*(2), 43-55.

Pinker, S. (2018). *Enlightenment Now.* Harlow, England: Penguin Books.

PLACES Lab. (2020, November 9). *USA Data: Land Value Maps.* Retrieved from PLACES Data Science for Conservation Decisions: https://web.archive.org/web/20210306051859/https://placeslab.org/fmv_us a/

Planes, A. (2013, September 30). *Was America's Budget Really Balanced in the '90's?* Retrieved from The Motley Fool: https://www.fool.com/investing/general/2013/09/30/was-americas-budget-really-balanced-in-the-90s.aspx

Plummer, E. (2010, March). Evidence on the Distributional Effects of a Land Value Tax on Residential Households. *National Tax Journal*, 63-92. doi:10.2307/41791102

Poverty in San Francisco | City Performance Scorecards. (2022, February). Retrieved from City and County of San Francisco: https://web.archive.org/web/20220104132749/https://sfgov.org/scorecards/safet y-net/poverty-san-francisco

PriceWaterHouseCoopers. (2006). *Retail Sales Tax Compliance Costs: A National Estimate.* PriceWaterHouseCoopers. Retrieved from http://www.netchoice.org/wp-content/uploads/cost-of-collection-study-sstp.pdf

Quote Investigator. (2016, February 5). *Riches Are Like Muck Which Stinks in a Heap But Spread Abroad*

Makes the Earth Fruitful. Retrieved from Quote
Investigator: https://quoteinvestigator.com/2016/
02/05/muck/

Raslanas, S., Zavadskas, E. K., Kaklauskas, A., & Zabulenas,
A. R. (2011, June 9). Land Value Tax in the Context
of Sustainable Urban Development and Assessment.
Part II - Analysis of Land Valuation Techniques: The
Case of Vilnius. *International Journal of Strategic
Property Management, 14*(2), 173-190.
doi:10.3846/ijspm.2010.13

Realtors® Land Institute. (2020). *The Land Report.*
Retrieved from LandReport.com: https://web.archive
.org/web/20220121084655/https://landreport.com/
americas-100-largest-landowners/

Reserve Bank of New Zealand. (2021, September 30). *Asset
Quality.* Retrieved from Bank Financial Strength
Dashboard: https://bankdashboard.rbnz.govt.nz/
asset-quality

Richter, F. (2020, September 4). *Up to 40 Million
Americans Face Eviction in 2020.* Retrieved from
Statista: https://web.archive.org/web/2021072902
2019/https://www.statista.com/chart/22385/evictio
n-crisis-us/

Roakes, S. L. (1996, October). Reconsidering land value
taxation: The golden key? *Land Use Policy, 13*(4),
261-272. doi:10.1016/0264-8377(96)84556-X

Rognlie, M. (2015). *Deciphering the Fall and Rise in the Net Capital Share: Accumulation or Scarcity?* Cambridge, Massachusetts: Massachusetts Institute of Technology.

Roser, M. (2017, December 2). *Fertility Rate.* Retrieved from Our World in Data: https://web.archive.org/web/20220207104701/https://ourworldindata.org/fertility-rate

Roser, M. (2019, November). *Future Population Growth.* Retrieved from Our World in Data: https://web.archive.org/web/20220212130206/https://ourworldindata.org/future-population-growth

Roser, M., & Ortiz-Ospina, E. (2013). *Global Extreme Poverty.* Retrieved from Our World in Data: https://web.archive.org/web/20220208000352/https://ourworldindata.org/extreme-poverty

Saez, E. a. (2016, May). Wealth Inequality in the United States Since 1913: Evidence from Capitalized Income Tax Data. *The Quarterly Journal of Economics, 131*(2), 521. Retrieved from https://web.archive.org/web/20210202081558/http:/gabriel-zucman.eu/files/SaezZucman2016QJE.pdf

Saez, E., & Zucman, G. (2014). *Wealth Inequality in the United States since 1913: Evidence from Capitalized Income Tax Data.* National Bureau of Economic Research.

Sale, K. (1995). *Rebels Against the Future: The Luddites and Their War on the Industrial Revolution.* Cambridge, Massachusetts: Perseus Publishing.

Schur, J. B. (2005, December). *Eli Whitney's Patent for the Cotton Gin.* Retrieved from National Archives Educator Resources: https://web.archive.org/web/20210203005127/https:/www.archives.gov/education/lessons/cotton-gin-patent

Seabury, C. (2020, September 15). *How Property Taxes Are Calculated.* Retrieved from Investopedia: https://web.archive.org/web/20201215230813/https:/www.investopedia.com/articles/tax/09/calculate-property-tax.asp

Shahbandeh, M. (2021, August 18). *Total Area of Land in United States Farms from 2000 to 2020 (in 1,000 acres).* Retrieved from Statista: https://www.statista.com/statistics/196104/total-area-of-land-in-farms-in-the-us-since-2000/

Shankar, P., Young, L., Haas, P., & Esling, P. (2019). *The Real Estate Mantra - Locate Near Public Transportation.* Washington, DC: American Public Transportation Association.

Shapiro, A. (2021, January 14). *America's Biggest Owner of Farmland Is Now Bill Gates.* Retrieved from Forbes: https://www.forbes.com/sites/arielshapiro/2021/01/14/americas-biggest-owner-of-farmland-is-now-bill-gates-bezos-turner/?sh=35c0e2e36096

Shokrizade, R. (2013, April 6). *How I used EVE Online to Predict the Great Recession.* Retrieved from GameDeveloper.com: https://web.archive.org/web/20220214085117/https://www.gamedeveloper.com/design/how-i-used-eve-online-to-predict-the-great-recession

SilverStar (2006, November 28). Illustration of Deadweight Loss Introduced by a (binding) Price Ceiling. Retrieved from https://commons.wikimedia.org/wiki/File:Deadweight-loss-price-ceiling.svg license: CC BY 2.5, https://creativecommons.org/licenses/by/2.5/legalcode

Skaburskis, A. (1995, August 1). The Consequence of Taxing Land Value. *Journal of Planning Literature, 10*(1), 3-21. doi:10.1177/088541229501000101

Smith, J. J. (2020). *Counting Bounty: The Quest to Know the Worth of Earth.* Chicago, Illinois: Trine Day LLC.

Smith, N. (2018, January 2). *Land Is Underrated as a Source of Wealth.* Retrieved from Blomberg Opinion: https://web.archive.org/web/20210416221923/https://www.bloomberg.com/opinion/articles/2018-01-02/land-is-underrated-as-a-source-of-wealth

St. Louis Fed. (2021, December 22). *Real Gross National Income.* Retrieved from FRED Economic Data: https://fred.stlouisfed.org/series/A023RX1Q020SBEA

Stevenson, A., & Li, C. (2021, December 9). *What to Know About China Evergrande, the Troubled Property Giant*. Retrieved from The New York Times: https://www.nytimes.com/article/evergrande-debt-crisis.html

Stevenson, R. (Director). (1964). *Mary Poppins* [Motion Picture].

Stiglitz, J. (1977). The Theory of Local Public Goods. *The Economcis of Public Services*, 274-333.

Stiglitz, J. E., & Arnott, R. J. (1979). Aggregate Land Rents, Expenditure on Public Goods, and Optimal City Size. *Quarterly Journal of Economics*, 471-500.

The_Great_Goblin. (2021, September 21). *Land value ownership inequality stats?* Retrieved from reddit.com/r/georgism: https://www.reddit.com/r/georgism/comments/pryhtf/land_value_ownership_inequality_stats/hdqf9m7/?context=3

Taylor, P. (2012, May 2). Park Place Expensive Real Estate Monopoly. Retrieved from https://www.flickr.com/photos/9731367@N02/6988181354 license: CC BY 2.0, https://creativecommons.org/licenses/by/2.0/, image modified from source

Tideman, N. (1990, November 7). Open Letter to Mikhail Gorbachev. Retrieved from https://en.wikisource.org/wiki/Open_letter_to_Mikhail_Gorbachev_(1990)

Tideman, N., Kumhof, M., Hudson, M., & Goodhart, C. (2021). Post-Corona Balanced-Budget Super-

Stimulus: The Case for Shifting Taxes onto Land. *CEPR Discussion Papers.*

U.S. Government Publishing Office. (2019). *An American Budget.* Washington, DC: U.S. Government Publishing Office.

USDA. (2020). *Land Values 2020 Summary.* Washington, DC: United States Department of Agriculture. Retrieved from https://www.nass.usda.gov/ Publications/Todays_Reports/reports/land0820.pdf

Various. (2021, February 22). *Native Americans Describe Traditional Views of Land Ownership.* Retrieved from SHEC: Resources for Teachers: https://web.archive.org/web/20210222090841/http s:/shec.ashp.cuny.edu/items/show/1543

Vaughan, G. (2021, September 23). *NZ Banks' Housing Lending Continues Rising as a Percentage of Their Overall Lending as Business and Agriculture :ending Heads in the Opposite Direction.* Retrieved from interest.co.nz: https://www.interest.co.nz/banking /112371/nz-banks-housing-lending-continues-rising-percentage-their-overall-lending-business

Vivier, T. L. (2017, January 26). *The Heartbreakingly Beautiful Story of the real 'Up house'.* Retrieved from Good Things Guy: https://web.archive.org/web/20201111163745/https: //www.goodthingsguy.com/people/house-inspired-disney/

Wealth and Want. (2006, May 24). *ATCOR: All Taxes Come Out of Rents*. Retrieved from Wealth and Want: http://www.wealthandwant.com/themes/ATCOR.html

Wedel, J. R. (1998, May 14). The Harvard Boys Do Russia. *The Nation*.

Woetzel, J., Mischke, J., Madgavkar, A., Windhagen, E., Smit, S., Birshan, M., . . . Anderson, R. J. (2021). *The Rise and Rise of the Global Balance Sheet: How Productively Are We Using Our Wealth?* McKinsey Global Institute.

Woo, A. (2016, June 14). *How Have Rents Changed Since 1960?* Retrieved from ApartmentList.com: https://www.apartmentlist.com/research/rent-growth-since-1960

Wyatt, M. D. (1994, March 1). A Critical View of Land Value Taxation as a Progressive Strategy for Urban Revitalization, Rational Land Use, and Tax Relief. *Review of Radical Political Economics, 26*(1), 1-25. doi:10.1177/048661349402600101

Xue, Y., Hu, Y., Yang, J., & Chen, Q. (2008). Land Evaluation Based on Boosting Decision Tree Ensembles. 78-81.

Yalpir, S., & Unel, F. B. (2017). Use of Spatial Analysis Methods in Land Appraisal; Konya Example. *5th International Symposium on Innovative Technologies in Engineering and Science*, 1574-1582. Baku, Azerbaijan. Retrieved from https://www.isites.info/

PastConferences/ISITES2017/ISITES2017/papers/
C3-ISITES2017ID307.pdf

Yglesias, M. (2013, December 20). *What's All the Land in America Worth?* Retrieved from SLATE: https://slate.com/business/2013/12/value-of-all-land-in-the-united-states.html

Printed in the USA
CPSIA information can be obtained
at www.ICGtesting.com
LVHW051923260724
786512LV00001B/16

9 798985 322521